lonely 🌐 p

T0047396

Florida &
the South's

NATIONAL PARKS

Contents

Plan Your Trip

Florida & the
South's National Parks
Top 12 4
Need to Know 12
Month by Month 14
Get Inspired 17
Health & Safety 18
Clothing &
Equipment 20
Florida & the
South's National
Parks Overview 22
Best Hiking 26
Best Flora
& Fauna 28
Best Family
Experiences 30
Best Adventures 32

Florida   35

Biscayne 38
Dry Tortugas 46

Everglades 48
Classic Drive: The
Everglades Tour 50

The South   55

Congaree 58
Great Smoky
Mountains 60
Hike: Alum
Cave Bluffs 66
Hike: Laurel Falls 67
Drive: Newfound
Gap Road 68
Drive: Roaring Forks
Motor Nature Trail 69
Classic Hike:
Charlies Bunion
& Kephart Loop 72
Classic Drive: Blue
Ridge Parkway Tour 74
Classic Drive:
Appalachian Trail 80
Hot Springs 86

In Focus

The Parks Today 108
History 110
Outdoor
Activities 116
Flora & Fauna 121
Conservation 127
Landscapes
& Geology 130
Index 134

Special Features

Florida Wildlife 42
Florida Flora 44
African American
Civil Rights
Network 104

Classic Drive: Natchez
Trace Parkway 90
Mammoth Cave 96
Classic Drive: Civil
Rights Tour 98

COVID-19

We have re-checked every business in this book before publication to ensure that it is still open after the COVID-19 outbreak. However, the economic and social impacts of COVID-19 will continue to be felt long after the outbreak has been contained, and many businesses, services and events referenced in this guide may experience ongoing restrictions. Some businesses may be temporarily closed, have changed their opening hours and services, or require bookings; some unfortunately could have closed permanently. We suggest you check with venues before visiting for the latest information.

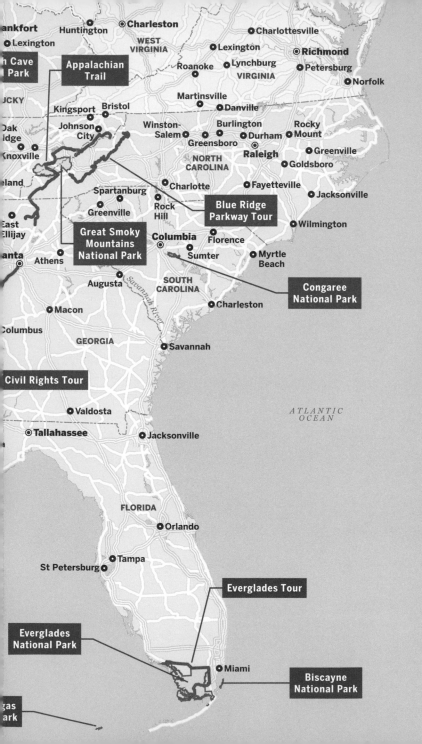

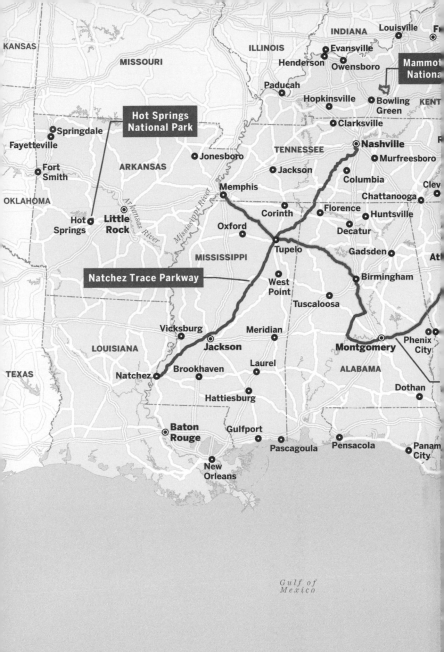

Welcome to Florida & the South's National Parks

National parks are the very essence of America; 63 superb, protected natural expanses that reflect this vast, complex and magnificently diverse country. You'll find some of the best parks down in Florida and the South.

National parks are America's big backyards, and no road trip would be complete without a visit to at least one of these natural treasures, rich in unspoiled wilderness, rare wildlife and history.

These parks represent American ideals at their best. That we're able to enjoy these special places today may seem routine, but the National Park System's establishment was no sure thing. Challenges have been present every step of the way, and many threatened to derail the entire experiment. So far, though, the best instincts of a nation have prevailed. And it's not just the national parks: there's also an incredible portfolio of federally protected areas that add depth and scale to your experience of wild America.

In fact, the region is so varied that it can seem at times as if all of America's natural beauty is crammed into one small corner of the country. There are the forests and mountains of Congaree and the Great Smoky Mountains, the subtropical wetlands of the Everglades, the healing waters of Hot Springs and America's biggest cave system at Mammoth Cave, not to mention underwater riches at Biscayne and Dry Tortugas.

The Blue Ridge Parkway and Great Smoky Mountains National Park may be America's most popular parks, and the state of Florida is certainly no stranger to development. But at the heart of this region's appeal is the call to wilderness in its parks: you'll find it in abundance here.

These parks represent American ideals at their best.

Snorkeling in Florida (p119)
EB ADVENTURE PHOTOGRAPHY/SHUTTERSTOCK ©

Roseate spoonbill, Everglades (p48).

Plan Your Trip
Florida & the South's National Parks Top 12

Paddling, Everglades

FINEPIC/SHUTTERSTOCK ©

The country's third-largest national park (p48) is a paddler's paradise, with kayak and canoe 'trails' meandering through mangrove swamps and freshwater marshes that feel like deep wilderness as soon as you cast off from one of the deserted shores. Navigating the waters is wonderfully straightforward thanks to the National Park Service's handy (and free) kayak and canoe trail maps.

DEAN FIKAR/SHUTTERSTOCK ©

Forests, Great Smoky Mountains

Wildlife isn't just about mammals, birds and reptiles (although the Great Smoky Mountains, p60, have these in abundance). It's Great Smoky's gloriously diverse forests that really make this park stand out: spruce and fir, pine and oak, hemlock and hardwoods – forests as far as the eye can see. Whether you're hiking through the shade of their canopies or gazing out over the forest-clad hillsides from a lookout, this is one of America's true botanical wonders.

PETER LEAHY/SHUTTERSTOCK ©

Coral Reefs, Biscayne

Florida's most breathtaking scenery is underwater. The peninsula is edged extensive coral reefs, and their quality and diversity rival Hawaii and the Caribbean. The prime protected areas are Biscayne National Park (p39), John Pennekamp Coral Reef State Park and Looe Key. You can see the reefs by snorkeling, diving and by glass-bottom boat, and also spend the night with the fish (at John Pennekamp) if you just can't bear to surface.

THIERRY EIDENWEIL/SHUTTERSTOCK ©

Wildlife Watching, Everglades

The Everglades (p48) is one of the US's great wildlife-watching destinations. You can reliably expect to see alligators and turtles, perhaps even soulful manatees if you know where to look, and you never quite know when and where you might see anything from a black bear to the elusive Florida panther. And this is prime bird-watching territory, with a remarkable variety of wading and shorebirds just about everywhere you go.

4

OGLETREE PHOTOGRAPHY/SHUTTERSTOCK ©

APPALACHIAN TRAIL APPROACH
SPRINGER MTN. GA. 8.5 MILES
MT. KATAHDIN MAINE 2190.9 MILES
BENTON MACKAYE TRAIL 8.7 MILES ◆
AMICALOLA FALLS
DAWSONVILLE GA.

Appalachian Trail

America's most fabled walk in the woods (p80) stretches for nearly 2200 miles across 14 states. Some 71 miles of the challenging trail runs along the spine of the Smoky Mountains, with soaring overlooks, misty coniferous forests, and fire towers offering staggering views over the verdant expanse. Even if you don't have a week to spare (much less six months to hike the whole thing), you can still enjoy some marvelous day or overnight hikes along this legendary trail.

5

Waterfalls, Great Smoky Mountains

Abundant rainfall and steep elevation provide the perfect ingredients for the Smoky Mountain's picturesque waterfalls. Thundering cascades are dotted all around, and some of the most popular hiking trails lead up to waterfalls, often surrounded by lush forest. If your time is limited, focus on one of the cascades near Gatlinburg. The stunning 80ft-high Rainbow Falls (p61) lives up to its name, with rainbows visible in the mist on sunny days.

6

WANGKUN JIA/SHUTTERSTOCK ©

KELLY VANDELLEN/SHUTTERSTOCK ©

Mammoth Cave, Kentucky

JUSTING88/SHUTTERSTOCK ©

There's something extraordinary about exploring the longest cave system on earth, and there are so many ways to do it. There are numerous tours (p96), and taking as many of these as you can is a superb way to get to know this astonishing subterranean world. Possibilities range from hour-long underground strolls to challenging, day-long spelunking adventures; the names of the tours tell a story in themselves: 'Frozen Niagara,' 'Domes & Dripstones' or the lantern-lit 'Violet City.'

7

Clingmans Dome, Great Smoky Mountains

The park's highest peak (p84) offers dazzling views; from the circular viewing platform you'll have a sweeping 360-degree panorama of the undulating forested peaks. It's an easy but steep uphill walk along the paved half-mile path to the observation tower, In winter, when the access road is closed, you'll have those grand views all to yourself.

Congaree National Park, South Carolina

Inky-black water, dyed with tannic acid from decaying plant matter. White cypress stumps like the femurs of long-dead giants. Moss as dry and gray as witches' hair. Congaree National Park (p58) has the largest old-growth bottomland forest in the eastern US, and canoeing through its unearthly swamp makes you feel like you've stepped into a Gothic novel.

CASELLEU/SHUTTERSTOCK ©

Dry Tortugas, Florida

Rather like the Florida Keys but even more removed from mainland USA, Dry Tortugas (p46) is a very long way from anywhere. This curious island outpost has deserted beaches (yes, in Florida!), incredible diving and snorkeling, rich bird-watching and a night sky that rivals anything the desert can offer. You can visit on a day trip, but you'll really capture the essence of its isolation if you stay overnight.

U! CREATIVE ©

Rafting the Pigeon River, Great Smoky Mountains

Drift between riverbanks cloaked in the Great Smoky Mountains' forests. If your idea of fun is a wild ride through untamed country, the challenging white water of the Upper Pigeon (p63) is the way to go. If you prefer something a little more sedate, choose the Lower Pigeon for a family-friendly journey with more beauty than adrenaline.

SEAN PAVONE/SHUTTERSTOCK ©

Hot Springs, Arkansas

One of the oldest and most celebrated spa centers in the South, Hot Springs National Park (p86) has a fabulous mix of thermal soaking fun and spa experiences along with historic Bathhouse Row and even the Gangster Museum. There's lots to see and do here on the margins of the springs, but the hot waters at the heart of this place will simply make you feel that all is right with the world.

12

Plan Your Trip
Need to Know

When to Go

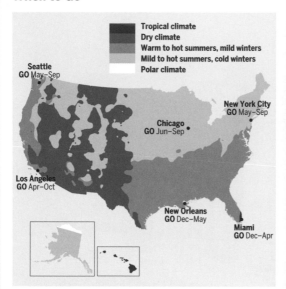

Tropical climate
Dry climate
Warm to hot summers, mild winters
Mild to hot summers, cold winters
Polar climate

Seattle
GO May–Sep

New York City
GO May–Sep

Chicago
GO Jun–Sep

Los Angeles
GO Apr–Oct

New Orleans
GO Dec–May

Miami
GO Dec–Apr

High Season (Mar–Aug)

◦ Hot and humid from May (to September).

◦ Florida beaches peak with spring break.

◦ Parks busy; book ahead for campgrounds, especially in July and August.

Shoulder (Feb & Sep)

◦ Waterfalls in Great Smoky Mountains are at their peak in spring.

◦ The weather in the Everglades is generally dry.

Low Season (mid-Sep–May)

◦ Hotel prices can drop from peak by 50%.

◦ November–April dry season is best time to hike/camp.

◦ High season for the subtropical Everglades.

Entry Fees

7-day pass from free to per vehicle/pedestrian $35/20.

America the Beautiful Annual Pass

$80 per vehicle valid for all national parks for 12 months from purchase. Buy through National Park Service (☎888-275-8747, ext 1; www.nps.gov).

ATMs

Most parks have at least one ATM; widely available in gateway towns.

Credit Cards

Major credit cards widely accepted; Forest Service, BLM and other campgrounds accept cash and/or checks only.

Cell Phones

Coverage inside parks is inconsistent at best.

Wi-fi

Some park lodges have wireless. Outside the parks, most cafes and hotels offer free wireless (chain hotels may charge).

Tipping

Tip restaurant servers 15–20%; porters $2 per bag; hotel maids $2 to $5 per night.

Advance Planning

Twelve months before Reserve campsites and historic lodge accommodations.
Six months before Reserve hotel rooms in satellite towns if visiting in summer. Book flights.
Three months before Start training if planning to backpack. If you haven't reserved sleeping arrangements, do so.
One month before Secure rental car. Take your own car in for a safety inspection and tune-up if planning a long drive.

Useful Websites

Lonely Planet (www.lonelyplanet.com/usa) Destination information, hotel reviews, traveler forum and more.
National Park Service (NPS; www.nps.gov) Gateway to America's greatest natural treasures, its national parks.
RoadsideAmerica.com (www.roadside america.com) Don't miss all those weird roadside attractions!
Florida State Parks (www.floridastate parks.org) Primary resource for state parks.
Visit Florida (www.visitflorida.com) Official state tourism website.

Accommodations

Campsites Reservation and first-come, first-served sites both available in all parks. Flush toilets are common, hot showers are not. Full hookups for RVs usually found outside parks.
Park Lodges Wonderful experiences. Usually lack TV; some have wi-fi.
B&Bs Available in gateway towns outside parks; often excellent and usually include wi-fi.
Hotels Occasionally inside parks; most in gateway towns. Nearly all have wi-fi.

Arriving at a National Park

Information Pick up a park newspaper at the entry kiosk and hang onto it; they're packed with useful information.
Camping If you're going for a first-come, first-served site, head straight to the

Daily Costs

Budget: Less than $150

- Camping & RV sites: $15–45
- Park entrance fee: free–$35
- Cheap self-catering food or cafe/diner meal: $6–15
- Park shuttles: free

Midrange: $150–250

- Double room in midrange hotel: $100–250
- Popular restaurant dinner for two: $30–60
- Car hire per day: from $30

Top end: More than $250

- Double room in a top-end hotel: from $200
- Dinner in a top restaurant: $60–100

campground. Try to arrive no later than mid-morning Friday.
Parking People not spending the night inside a park will find parking difficult. Arrive early, park and take free shuttles whenever possible.
Visitor Centers Best places to start exploring the parks. Purchase books and maps, ask rangers questions, check weather reports and trail and road conditions.

Getting Around

Car Most convenient way to travel between the parks. A few park roads are gravel. Traffic inside some parks can be horrendous.

Park Shuttles Many parks have excellent shuttle systems with stops at major visitor sites and trailheads.

Bicycles Some parks have rentals. Good for getting around developed areas. Elsewhere, roads can be steep and shoulders narrow.

14

Plan Your Trip
Month by Month

January
January falls in the middle of Florida's winter 'dry' season. In northern Florida, cool temps make this low season. Down south, the subtropical Everglades are sublime.

February
Up north the crowds are thin, the air is still crisp and the days are short; it's a good time for travel discounts just about everywhere

✕ Everglades Seafood Festival
At the height of the stone crab season, Everglades City celebrates Gulf seafood over three days with fabulous feasts and live music.

March
The first blossoms of spring arrive (at least in the South), and it can be a lovely time to be in the Everglades, Biscayne or the Dry Tortugas. Drunken spring breakers descend on Florida.

✿ Spring Break
Throughout March to mid-April, American colleges release students for one-week 'spring breaks.' Coeds pack Florida beaches for debaucherous drunken binges. The biggies? Panama City Beach, Pensacola, Daytona and Fort Lauderdale. Avoid or join in as is your pleasure.

✿ Gainesville Native American Festival
This fun little festival celebrates north-central Florida's Native American heritage with food, crafts and performances over a March weekend.

April
Wildflowers are in full swing at lower elevations, and waterfalls start pumping at peak force with the beginning of snowmelt. It's a mighty fine time to travel down south.

Above: Everglades Seafood Festival

🏃 National Park Week

For an entire week every April, admission to national parks is free. Early in the year, the US president announces when National Park Week will fall that year. Many of the parks also host free activities.

May

Temperatures ramp up but summer crowds are yet to materialize in the parks. A lovely time to travel all round.

🏃 Sea Turtle Nesting

Beginning in May and extending through October, sea turtles nest on Florida beaches; after two months (from midsummer through fall) hatchling runs see the kids totter back to sea.

June

It's still possible to beat the summer crowds in early June. By late June, parks are jammed but the weather is stellar in many of them, especially the Great Smoky Mountains.

★ Top Events

National Park Week, April

Summer Wildflowers, July

Sea Turtle Nesting, May

Mountain Life Festival, September

Everglades Seafood Festival, February

📅 Hurricane Season

June marks the start of hurricane season. Whenever a storm's approaching, it will be all over the news, giving you time to get out of the way. Florida is on the front line, but hurricanes can hit anywhere in the South. The season peaks in September/October.

July

It's prime hiking time in the high country of the Great Smoky Mountains, though crowds are at their peak. It's damned hot in Florida.

Above: Sea turtle hatchlings

☉ Summer Wildflowers

There's nothing like hiking through high-country meadows blanketed in wildflowers. In the Great Smoky Mountains, wildflowers bloom intensely during the short growing season that begins in June and peaks in July.

August

Hello crowds! It's the height of summer, it's blazing hot and every hotel and campsite is reserved. First-come, first-served camp-grounds are your best bet. Avoid the humid Everglades and head to Biscayne's waters or the Great Smoky Mountains, where the weather is superb.

September

The crowds begin to thin, and by the end of the month things are pretty quiet. If you don't mind brisk evenings, this can be a beautiful time to visit the parks. Florida's south starts to become bearable again.

✤ Mountain Life Festival

Participate in hearth cooking demonstra-tions and help make historic farm staples like hominy, apple butter, apple cider and soap. The event is celebrated every year in mid-September at the Mountain Farm Museum in the Great Smoky Mountains National Park.

October

In the Great Smoky Mountains, the fall colors are nothing short of fabulous. Crowds are nonexistent and the temperatures are dropping quickly.

November

Winter is creeping in quickly in the South and elsewhere, but Florida's south is glorious as its winter 'dry' season begins. Thanksgiving holidays see a tourism spike for a week.

✤ Fall Country Jamboree

Barberville in north-central Florida is the cracker (rural Floridian) heartland, and on November's first weekend the Fall Country Jamboree host Florida's best pioneer-heritage festival, with folk music and demonstrations of cracker life.

December

Winter is well underway in most of the parks, but it's high season down in the Everglades. Elsewhere across Georgia, Alabama and the Carolinas, visitor center and business hours are reduced.

✤ National Audubon Society Christmas Bird Count

Every year around Christmastime, thou-sands of people take to the wilds to look for and record birds for the Audubon Society's annual survey. Many of the parks organize a count and rely on volunteers to help. Check the National Park Service websites for information.

Plan Your Trip
Get Inspired

MAXIMUM FILM/ALAMY STOCK PHOTO ©

Read

Where the Crawdads Sing (Delia Owens; 2018) Murder mystery that beautifully depicts the essence of the wild and human South.

Salvaging the Real Florida (Bill Belleville; 2011) Moving nature essays on a fragile landscape.

Wildlife in America (Peter Matthiessen; 1959) A classic about America's wildlife story.

Cat Tale (Craig Pittman; 2020) The quirky story of the fight to save the Florida panther from extinction.

Watch

Scarface (1983) Al Pacino finds the American Dream. Sort of.

There's Something about Mary (1998) A Miami-set comedy of errors.

Key Largo (1948) A classic of Sunshine State noir.

Listen

Classic Old-Time Fiddle (2007) Perfect fiddle compilation for trips to the Great Smoky Mountains.

Anthology of American Folk Music (1952) Ideal blues, folk and country for Tennessee and the South.

Southern Accents (1995) Pick any album by native son Tom Petty and you'll endear yourself to Gators fans.

Beautiful Maladies (1998) Nothing spells 'road trip' like a good Tom Waits tune.

This Land Is Your Land: The Asch Recordings, Vol. 1 (1997) Woody Guthrie sings everything from 'This Land Is Your Land' to 'The Car Song.'

Plan Your Trip
Health & Safety

Before You Go

If you require medications bring them in their original, labeled containers. A signed and dated letter from your physician describing your medical conditions and medications, including generic names, is a good idea. If carrying syringes or needles, be sure to have a physician's letter documenting their necessity.

Some of the walks in this book are physically demanding and most require a reasonable level of fitness. Even if you're tackling the easy or easy-to-moderate walks, it pays to be relatively fit, rather than launch straight into them after months of fairly sedentary living. If you're aiming for the demanding walks, fitness is essential.

If you have any medical problems, or are concerned about your health in any way, it's a good idea to have a full checkup before you start walking.

In the Parks

Visiting city dwellers will need to keep their wits about them in order to minimize the chances of suffering an avoidable accident or tragedy. Dress appropriately, tell people where you are going, don't bite off more than you can chew and, above all, respect the wilderness and the inherent dangers that it conceals.

Crime is far more common in big cities than in sparsely populated national parks. Nevertheless, use common sense: lock valuables in the trunk of your vehicle, especially if you're parking it at a trailhead overnight, and never leave anything worth stealing in your tent.

Walk Safety – Basic Rules

● Allow plenty of time to accomplish a walk before dark, particularly when daylight hours are shorter.

● Study the route carefully before setting out, noting the possible escape routes and the point of no return (where it's quicker to continue than to turn back). Monitor your progress during the day against the time estimated for the walk, and keep an eye on the weather.

o It's wise not to walk alone. Always leave details of your intended route, the number of people in your group and your expected return time with someone responsible before you set off, and let that person know when you return.

o Before setting off, make sure you have a relevant map, compass and whistle, and that you know the weather forecast for the area for the next 24 hours. In mountainous areas always carry extra warm, dry layers of clothing and plenty of emergency high-energy food.

Altitude

Although most of Florida and the South is fairly low in altitude, being at altitude affects travelers in different ways. The highest point you're likely to reach is Clingmans Dome (6643ft) in the Great Smoky Mountains. At that elevation you shouldn't encounter any problems, but it still helps to know what to do if you come into difficulties.

o Ascend slowly – have frequent rest days, spending two to three nights at each rise of 3281ft (1000m).

o It is always wise to sleep at a lower altitude than the greatest height reached during the day, if possible.

o Drink extra fluids. The mountain air is dry and cold and moisture is lost as you breathe; evaporation of sweat may occur unnoticed and result in dehydration.

o Eat light, high-carbohydrate meals for more energy.

o Avoid alcohol and sedatives.

★ Water Purification

To ensure you are getting safe, clean drinking water in the backcountry you have three basic options:

Boiling Water is considered safe to drink if it has been boiled at 212°F (100°C) for at least a minute. This is best done when you set up your camp and stove in the evening.

Chemical Purification There are two types of chemical additives that will purify water: chlorine or iodine. You can choose from various products on the market. Read the instructions carefully first, be aware of expiration dates and check you are not allergic to either chemical.

Filtration Mobile devices can pump water through microscopic filters and take out potentially harmful organisms. If carrying a filter, take care it doesn't get damaged in transit, read the instructions carefully and always filter the cleanest water you can find.

Rescue & Evacuation

If someone in your group is injured or falls ill and can't move, leave somebody with them while one or more other people go for help. They should take clear written details of the location and condition of the victim, and of helicopter landing conditions. If there are only two of you, leave the injured person with as much warm clothing, food and water as it's sensible to spare, plus the whistle and torch. Mark the position with something conspicuous – an orange bivvy bag, or perhaps a large stone cross on the ground.

Top left: Appalachian Trail sign

Plan Your Trip
Clothing & Equipment

LL28/GETTY IMAGES ©

Deciding what gear is essential for a trip and what will only weigh you down is an art. Smartphone apps, new filtration systems and battery chargers are changing the game. Don't forget essentials, but be ruthless when packing, since every ounce counts.

Layering

The secret to comfortable walking is to wear several layers of light clothing, which you can easily take off or put on as you warm up or cool down. Most walkers use three main layers: a base layer next to the skin; an insulating layer; and an outer-shell layer for protection from wind, rain and snow.

For the upper body, the base layer is typically a shirt of synthetic material that wicks moisture away from the body and reduces chilling. The insulating layer retains heat next to your body, and is usually a (windproof) fleece jacket or sweater. The outer shell consists of a waterproof jacket that also protects against cold wind.

For the lower body, the layers generally consist of either shorts or loose-fitting trousers, thermal underwear ('long johns') and waterproof overtrousers.

When purchasing outdoor clothing, one of the most practical fabrics is merino wool. Though pricier than other materials, natural wool absorbs sweat, retains heat even when wet, and is soft and comfortable to wear. Even better, it doesn't store odors like other sports garments, so you can wear it for several days in a row without inflicting antisocial smells on your tent mates.

Waterproof Shells

Jackets should be made of a breathable, waterproof fabric, with a hood that is roomy enough to cover headwear, but that still allows peripheral vision. Other handy features include underarm zippers for easy ventilation and a large map pocket with a heavy-gauge zipper protected by a storm flap.

Waterproof pants are best with slits for pocket access and long leg zips so that you can pull them on and off over your boots.

Footwear

Running shoes are OK for walks that are graded easy or moderate. However, you'll probably appreciate, if not need, the support and protection provided by hiking boots for more demanding walks. Nonslip soles (such as Vibram) provide the best grip.

Buy boots in warm conditions or go for a walk before trying them on, so that your feet can expand slightly, as they would on a hike. It's also a good idea to carry a pair of sandals to wear at night for getting in and out of tents easily or at rest stops. Sandals are also useful when fording waterways.

Gaiters help to keep your feet dry in wet weather and on boggy ground; they can also deflect small stones or sand and maintain leg warmth. The best are made of strong fabric, with a robust zip protected by a flap, and secure easily around the foot.

Walking socks should be free of ridged seams in the toes and heels.

Backpack & Daypacks

For day walks, a daypack (30L to 40L) will usually suffice, but for multiday walks you will need a backpack of between 45L and 90L capacity. Even if the manufacturer claims your pack is waterproof, use heavy-duty liners.

Bear Spray

There are small populations of black bear across Florida, Georgia, Alabama and Mississippi, so keep an eye out if you're hiking through bear country. Bear spray (pepper spray) can be used to deter aggressive bears, and park authorities often recommend that you equip yourself with a canister when venturing into backcountry. Familiarize yourself with the manufacturer's instructions before use, and only use as a last resort (ie on a charging bear 30ft

to 50ft away from you). Buy it from shops in or around parks, or online (it costs about $35 to $45). It's best kept close at hand on a belt around your waist.

Tent

A three-season tent will fulfill most walkers' requirements. The floor and the outer shell, or fly, should have taped or sealed seams and covered zips to stop leaks. The weight can be as low as 2.2lb (1kg) for a stripped-down, low-profile tent, and up to 6.6lb (3kg) for a roomy, luxury, four-season model.

Dome- and tunnel-shaped tents handle windy conditions better than flat-sided tents.

Map & Compass

You should always carry a good map of the area in which you are walking, and know how to read it. Before setting off on your walk, ensure that you are aware of the contour interval, the map symbols, the magnetic declination (difference between true and grid north), plus the main ridge and river systems in the area and the general direction in which you are heading. On the trail, try to identify major landforms such as mountain ranges and valleys, and locate them on your map to familiarize yourself with the geography.

Buy a compass and learn how to use it. The attraction of magnetic north varies in different parts of the world, so compasses need to be balanced accordingly. Compass manufacturers have divided the world into five zones. Make sure your compass is balanced for your destination zone. There are also 'universal' compasses on the market that can be used anywhere in the world.

Top left: Hiker, Great Smoky Mountains (p60)

Florida & the South's National Parks Overview

NAME	STATE	ENTRANCE FEE
Biscayne National Park (p38)	Florida	Free
Congaree National Park (p58)	South Carolina	Free
Dry Tortugas National Park (p46)	Florida	7-day pass per person $15
Everglades National Park (p48)	Florida	7-day pass per vehicle $25
Great Smoky Mountains National Park (p60)	North Carolina & Tennessee	Free
Hot Springs National Park (p86)	Arkansas	Free
Mammoth Cave National Park (p96)	Kentucky	Free; cave tours $6-60

Other NPS-Designated Sites & Areas

NAME	STATE	DESIGNATION
Little Rock Central High School (p104)	Arkansas	National Historic Site
Lorraine Motel (p105)	Tennessee	African American Civil Rights Network
Medgar & Myrlie Evers Home (p105)	Mississippi	National Monument
Penn Center (p104)	South Carolina	Reconstruction Era National Historical Park

DESCRIPTION	GREAT FOR...
A portion of the world's third-largest reef sits here off the coast of Florida, along with mangrove forests and the Florida Keys.	
The lush trees growing here are some of the tallest in the eastern USA, forming one of the highest temperate deciduous forest canopies left in the world.	
Your efforts to get here (by boat or plane only) will be rewarded with amazing snorkeling, diving, bird-watching and stargazing.	
This is not just a wetland, or a swamp, or a lake, or a river, or a prairie, or a grassland – it is all of the above.	
The iconic Great Smoky Mountains National Park offers visitors a chance to experience deep, mysterious old-growth forests.	
Hot Springs borders a city that has made an industry out of the park's major resource: mineral-rich waters.	
With hidden underground rivers and more than 400 miles of explored terrain, the world's longest cave system shows off sci-fi-looking stalactites and stalagmites up close.	

DESCRIPTION
The site of the 1957 desegregation crisis that changed the country forever.
Where Martin Luther King Jr was fatally shot on April 4, 1968.
The ranch-style home where Civil Rights activist Medgar Evers was murdered in 1963.
Once the home of one of the nation's first schools for freed slaves.

Road Trips

NAME	STATE	DISTANCE/DURATION
Appalachian Trail (p80)	Georgia–Tennessee	343 miles / 5–7 days
Blue Ridge Parkway Tour (p74)	Virginia–North Carolina	210 miles / 5 days
Civil Rights Tour (p98)	Georgia–Tennessee	568 miles / 4 days
Natchez Trace Parkway (p90)	Tennessee–Mississippi	444 miles / 3 days
The Everglades Tour (p50)	Florida	170 miles / 2–3 days

DESCRIPTION	ESSENTIAL PHOTO
Georgia, Tennessee and North Carolina each claim a section of the 2175-mile Maine-to-Georgia trail. On this journey you'll get a taste of the trail and the charming towns alongside it.	Max Patch Mountain offers signature views of the lower portion of the AT.
This drive on the USA's favorite byway – an NPS-designated national parkway – curves through the leafy Appalachians, where it swoops up the East Coast's highest peak and stops by the nation's largest mansion.	The mile-high suspension bridge at Grandfather Mountain.
Feel and absorb the history of the American Civil Rights movement as you follow in the footsteps of the legendary Dr Martin Luther King Jr from Atlanta to Memphis, including a range of NPS-designated historic sites and monuments.	The Edmund Pettus Bridge at sunset has an eerie, solemn beauty.
With emerald mounds, opulent mansions and layers of American history, the Natchez Trace Parkway winds 444 gorgeously wooded miles from Nashville all the way to southern Mississippi.	Emerald Mound, the second-largest Native American mound in the world, just before sunset.
Wade into the Everglades' vast 'river of grass,' where alligators float through mangrove swamps, birds soar across flooded horizons and endangered manatees perform elegant underwater ballet in the bays.	Alligators lounging in the sun at Shark Valley.

Plan Your Trip
Best Hiking

Above: Linville Falls; Top left: Mt LeConte; Top right: Alum Cave Trail

Nothing encapsulates the spirit of the national parks like hiking. Thousands of miles of trails crisscross the parks, offering access to their most scenic mountain passes, highest waterfalls and quietest corners.

Alum Cave Bluffs, Great Smoky Mountains

Climb past bubbling brooks and through glorious forests in one of Great Smoky's best trails.

Oakridge Trail, Congaree

A classic of the Carolinas, this trail is wonderfully scenic and the pick of Congaree's forest-and-stream paths.

Charlies Bunion & Kephart Loop, Great Smoky Mountains

One of few multiday hiking possibilities in the parks of Florida and the South (unless you count the Appalachian Trail), and it's a brilliant walk.

Mt LeConte, Great Smoky Mountains

Take one of five trails to the summit of Mt LeConte and enjoy some of the best views in Great Smoky.

Rainbow Falls Trail, Great Smoky Mountains

Hike through old-growth forest to one of the prettiest waterfalls you'll see anywhere.

Linville Falls, Blue Ridge Parkway

The pick of many short trails along the Blue Ridge Parkway, this one combines accessibility with stunning waterfalls.

Plan Your Trip
Best Flora & Fauna

Above: Alligator (p43); Top right: Great Smoky Mountains (p60); Bottom right: Black bear cubs (p122)

Florida and the South are home to charismatic creatures both great and small, and the diversity of its forests and plant life is almost unrivaled in the US.

Anhinga Trail, Everglades

Spot alligators soaking up the sun and watch for the trail's namesake birds as they spear their prey with their razor-sharp bills.

Flamingo Marina, Everglades

Watch as manatees roll and play and just hang out right alongside the marina. You can see manatees elsewhere in Florida, but not like here.

Maritime Heritage Trail, Biscayne

Explore the extraordinarily rich marine life of Biscayne National Park on this trail through sunken wrecks. Diving and snorkeling are both possible.

Black Bears, Great Smoky Mountains

There are black bears all over America's South, but the backcountry hiking trails of the Great Smoky Mountains are your best chance for an encounter.

Forests, Great Smoky Mountains

Hardwoods and hemlock, pine and oak. There's almost nowhere else in the US with the botanical variety of the Great Smoky Mountains.

Plan Your Trip
Best Family Experiences

Above: Mammoth Cave (p96); Top right: Hot Springs (p86); Bottom right: Steam train (p75), Blue Ridge Parkway

There's something inherently uplifting about bringing kids to national parks, most of which offer educational programs and activities designed to engage children in the environments around them.

Cave Tour, Mammoth Cave

Longer than any other known cave, with vast interior cathedrals, bottomless pits and strange, undulating rock formations.

Pigeon River, Great Smoky Mountains

Raft down the relatively gentle waters of the Lower Pigeon River, with time to enjoy the beautiful scenery along the way.

Hot Springs National Park

It doesn't matter how old you are; the whole family can enjoy the restorative powers of the Hot Springs National Park.

Blue Ridge Parkway

Ride in a steam train or an aerial tramway, look for gemstones and enjoy family-fun activities along this classic US road trip.

Fontana Lake, Great Smoky Mountains

Paddle the quiet and tranquil waters of this popular spot; it's one of few places where you can get out on the water in this stunning park.

Scenic Drive, Great Smoky Mountains

You don't even have to leave the car to get a fantastic overview of what this amazing park has to offer; the passing views are sure to get the kids looking up from their iPads.

Plan Your Trip
Best Adventures

Above: Great Smoky Mountains (p60); Top left: Kayaking (p48), Everglades; Top right: Appalachian Trail (p80)

With environments ranging from the subtropics of the Everglades to the mountains and deep forests of the Great Smoky Mountains, the national parks of Florida and the South have no shortage of spectacular settings for a bit of adventure.

Hiking, Appalachian Trail

One of America's most storied long-distance hikes, the Appalachian Trail covers almost 2200 miles. Hiking the whole thing is a six-month undertaking, but there are many wonderful day and overnight hikes to enjoy.

Paddling, Everglades

Paddle the 99-mile Wilderness Waterway, a labyrinth of mangroves, swamps and the waterways of the 10,000 Islands.

Canoeing, Congaree

Leave the crowds behind on the 27-mile Wilderness Canoe Tour, a seasonal exploration of the forest-lined backwaters of this pretty park. There's no better way to escape the crowds.

Hiking, Great Smoky Mountains

The Great Smoky Mountains National Park is one of America's busiest, and the 14.1-mile overnight Charlies Bunion & Kephart Loop hike is the ideal way to leave 99% of the park's visitors behind.

FLORIDA

In This Chapter

Biscayne 38
Dry Tortugas 46
Everglades 48

Florida

The only tropical state in the contiguous US is the domain of alligators, manatees, panthers and flamingos, as well as an abundance of well-protected coral reefs teeming with marine life. Three national parks inhabit America's beloved 'sunshine state': the mangrove-covered Everglades, the largely subaqueous Biscayne and the splayed keys of Dry Tortugas, which – unusually for a US national park – are guarded by a huge 19th-century military complex.

Don't Miss

o Diving to sunken ships on Biscayne's Maritime Heritage Trail (p39)

o Flying or sailing out to the remote key of Fort Jefferson (p46)

o Going on a self-guided paddle through the famously vast Everglades (p48)

o Finding an isolated island spot in Biscayne to pitch your tent (p39)

o Reptile-spotting on the short, paved Anhinga Trail (p48)

When to Go

In contrast to most other US national parks, Florida's trio of parks are best visited during the winter dry season (December to March) when there's top wildlife viewing along the watercourses of the Everglades (although some kayaking routes will be difficult).

Between April and June the weather gets pretty hot, but there's a good mix of water and wildlife. From July to November the heat increases, bringing with it lots of bugs and chances of hurricanes.

Previous page: Everglades National Park (p48)
LIGA CERINA/SHUTTERSTOCK ©

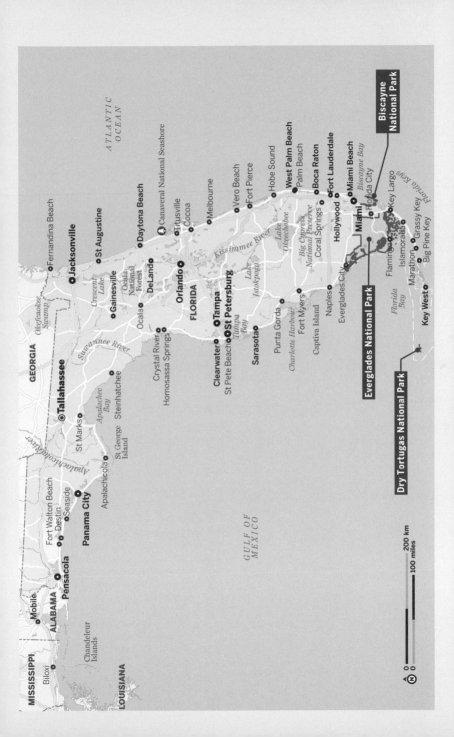

PIXELPOD / ALAMY STOCK PHOTO ©

Biscayne National Park

Just to the east of the Everglades is Biscayne National Park, or the 5% of it that isn't underwater. In fact, a portion of the world's third-largest reef sits here off the coast of Florida, along with mangrove forests and the northernmost Florida Keys.

Great For...

State
Florida

Entrance Fee
Free

Area
270 sq miles

Boating

Boating is naturally very popular, but you'll need to get some paperwork in order. Boaters will want to obtain tide charts from the park (or from www.nps.gov/bisc/planyourvisit/tide-predictions.htm). Also make sure you comply with local slow-speed zones, designed to protect the endangered manatee. If you'd like a guided paddle, or if you'd rather be taking in the scenery than tending the helm, take one of the boat tours with the **Biscayne National Park Institute** (☎786-335-3644; www.biscaynenationalparkinstitute.org; Dante Fascell Visitor Center; ⊙9am-5pm Wed-Sun) or another authorised operator.

The water around Convoy Point is regarded as prime windsurfing territory. Windsurfers may want to contact outfits in Miami.

Diving

The **Maritime Heritage Trail** takes divers through one of the only trails of its kind in the USA. If you've ever wanted to explore a sunken ship, this may well be the best opportunity in the country. Six are located within the park grounds; the trail experience involves taking visitors out, by boat, to the site of the wrecks where they can swim and explore among derelict vessels and clouds of fish.

There are even waterproof information site cards placed among the ships. Three of the vessels are suited for scuba divers, but the others – particularly the *Mandalay*, a lovely two-masted schooner that sank in 1966 – can be accessed by snorkelers.

Camping

Biscayne National Park's two **campgrounds** (site per night $25, May-Sep free) are

Essential Information

Dante Fascell Visitor Center (☏305-230-1144; www.nps.gov/bisc; 9700 SW 328th St, Homestead; ☉9am-5pm) Located at Convoy Point, this center shows a great introductory film for an overview of the park, and has maps, information and excellent ranger activities.

To get to the park, you'll have to drive about 9 miles east of Homestead on SW 328th St (North Canal Dr).

both located on islands – Elliott Key and Boca Chita Key. These are lovely settings, but you need transportation (a boat) to get there. You pay on a trust system with exact change on the harbor (rangers cruise the Keys to check your receipt). Bring all supplies, including water, and carry everything out. ∎

Top left: Butterfly fish, Biscayne National Park (p38); Bottom left: Anhinga, Biscayne National Park

TOM STACK/ALAMY STOCK PHOTO ©

ARTHURGPHOTOGRAPHY/SHUTTERSTOCK ©

PIXELPOD/ALAMY STOCK PHOTO ©

Top right: Lighthouse, Boca Chita Key (p39); Bottom right: Boating, Biscayne National Park (p38)

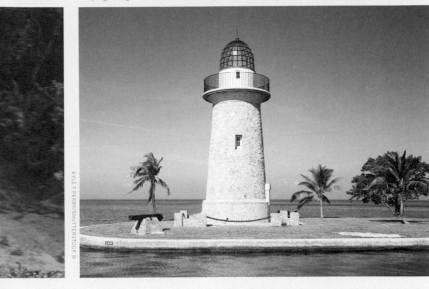

KYLE T PERRY/SHUTTERSTOCK ©

Florida Wildlife

With swamps full of gators, rivers full of snakes, manatees in mangroves, sea turtles on beaches, and giant flocks of seabirds taking wing at once, how is it, again, that a squeaky-voiced mouse became Florida's headliner? Florida has wonderful wildlife, both in terms of numbers and sheer variety. You just need to know where to look.

For more wildlife, see p121.

Manatees

It's hard to believe Florida's West Indian manatees were ever mistaken for mermaids, but it's easy to see their attraction: these gentle, curious, colossal mammals are as sweetly lovable as 10ft, 1500lb teddy bears.

Florida Panthers

Florida's most endangered mammal is the Florida panther, which was hunted relentlessly until 1958. A captive breeding program has saved them from extinction, but there are still as few as 130 known to exist.

Florida Black Bears

Florida black bears have a population of around 3000 to 4000; as their forests diminish, they're occasionally seen traipsing through suburbs in northern Florida.

Sea Turtles

Loggerhead, green and leatherback turtles create more than 80,000 nests annually on Florida's beaches.

American Alligators

American alligators are ubiquitous in central and southern Florida; while they don't pose much of a threat to humans, you should avoid feeding, provoking or stepping on them and it's a good idea to keep small children and pets away from unfamiliar inland bodies of water.

Florida Flora

What Florida lacks in topographical variety, it more than makes up for in plant diversity. The varied nature of the peninsula's flora, including more than 4000 species of plants, is unmatched in the continental US.

For more flora, see p124.

Ghost Orchid

Florida has more species of orchids than any other state in the US, and the Florida orchid that inspires the most intense devotion is the rare ghost orchid.

Mangroves

Where not shaved smooth by sand, southern Florida's coastline is often covered with a three-day stubble of mangroves.

Swamp Flowers

Florida's swamps are abundant with rooted plants with floating leaves, including the pretty American lotus, water lilies and spatterdock.

Bald Cypress

A dramatic, beautiful tree found in Florida's swamps, the bald cypress is the world's most flood-tolerant.

Sea Oats

Sea oats, with large plumes that trap windblown sand, are important for stabilizing coastal dunes.

Fort Jefferson

Dry Tortugas National Park

Dry Tortugas National Park is America's most inaccessible national park. Reachable only by boat or seaplane, it rewards you for your effort in getting there with amazing snorkeling amid coral reefs full of marine life. You'll also get to tour a beautifully preserved 19th-century brick fort, one of the largest in the USA.

Great For...

State
Florida

Entrance Fee
7-day pass per person $15

Area
100 sq miles

Fort Jefferson

Explorer Ponce de León named this seven-island chain Las Tortugas (The Turtles) for the sea turtles spotted in its waters. Thirsty mariners who passed through and found no water later affixed 'dry' to the name. In subsequent years, the US Navy set an outpost here as a strategic position into the Gulf of Mexico. But by the Civil War, Fort Jefferson, the main structure on the islands, had become a prison for Union deserters and at least four other people, among them Dr Samuel Mudd, who had been arrested for complicity in the assassination of Abraham Lincoln. Hence a new nickname: Devil's Island. The name was prophetic: in 1867 a yellow-fever outbreak killed 38 people, and after an 1873 hurricane the fort was abandoned. It reopened in 1886 as a quarantine station for smallpox and cholera victims, was declared a national monument in 1935 by President Franklin D Roosevelt, and was

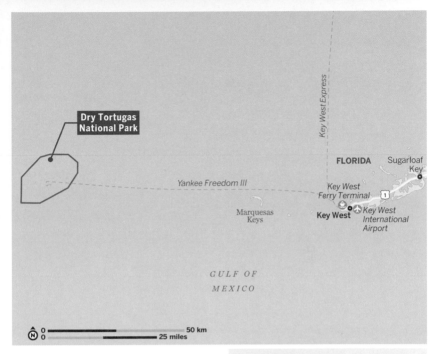

Dry Tortugas National Park

Key West Express

FLORIDA   Sugarloaf Key

Yankee Freedom III

Key West Ferry Terminal

Marquesas Keys

Key West   Key West International Airport

GULF OF MEXICO

0   50 km
0   25 miles

upped to national park status in 1992 by George Bush Sr.

Other Activities

The sparkling waters offer excellent snorkeling and diving opportunities. A visitor center is located within fascinating Fort Jefferson.

In March and April, there is stupendous bird-watching, including aerial fighting. Stargazing is mind-blowing at any time of the year.

Camping

You can come for the day or overnight if you want to camp. Garden Key has 10 campsites ($15 per person, per night), which are given out on a first-come, first-served basis. You'll need to reserve months ahead through the ferry *Yankee Freedom III,* which takes passengers to and from the island. There are toilets, but

Essential Information

The **Yankee Freedom III** (☑800-634-0939; www.drytortugas.com; 100 Grinell St; adult/child/senior $180/125/170) runs between the Key West Ferry Terminal and Fort Jefferson. Round-trip fares cost $180/125 per adult/child and the journey takes just over two hours.

Key West Seaplanes (☑305-293-9300; www.keywestseaplanecharters.com; half-day trip adult/child $342/273, full-day trip $600/480) can take up to 10 passengers (flight time 40 minutes each way) and departs frome near the Key West International Airport. The half-day tour is four hours, allowing 2½ hours on the island. The eight-hour full-day excursion gives you six hours on the island.

no freshwater showers or drinking water; bring everything you'll need. You can stay up to four nights. ∎

ROMRODPHOTO/SHUTTERSTOCK ©

Everglades National Park

This vast wilderness, encompassing 1.5 million acres, is one of America's great natural treasures. Spy alligators basking in the noonday sun as herons stalk patiently through nearby waters in search of prey, or go kayaking amid tangled mangrove canals and on peaceful lakes,

Great For...

State
Florida

Entrance Fee
7-day pass per vehicle/pedestrian
$25/8

Area
2344 sq miles

Anhinga Trail

If you do just one walk in the Everglades, make sure it's on the Anhinga Trail. Gators sun on the shoreline, anhinga spear their prey and wading birds stalk haughtily through the reeds. You'll get a close-up view of wildlife on this short (0.8-mile) trail at the Royal Palm Visitor Center, four miles from the main park entrance and the **Ernest Coe Visitor Center** (☎305-242-7700; www.nps.gov/ever; ☺8am-7pm mid-December to mid-April, from 9am rest of year). There are various overlooks, where you can sometimes see dozens of alligators piled together in the day.

Canoes, Kayaks & Bicycles

You need a car to properly enter the Everglades and once you're in, wearing a good pair of walking boots is essential to penetrate the interior. Having a canoe or kayak helps as well; these can be rented

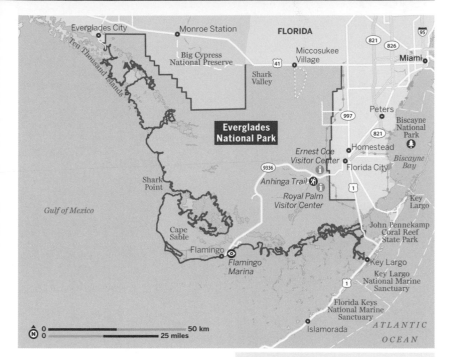

from outfits inside and outside the park, or else you can seek out guided canoe and kayak tours. Bicycles are well suited to the flat roads here, particularly in the area between Ernest Coe and Flamingo Point.

The most isolated portion of the park is squat **Flamingo Marina** (☎855-798-2207; www.flamingoeverglades.com; tours per adult/child $38/18, canoe rental 2/4/8hr $20/28/38, kayak rental half/full day $35/45; ⊙marina 7am-7pm, from 6am Sat & Sun) where you can go on a backcountry boat tour or rent boats. You can rent kayaks and canoes here; if you do, you're largely left to explore the channels and islands of Florida Bay on your own.

Southern Everglades

Head south of Miami to drive into the heart of the park and the best horizons of the Everglades. Plus there are plenty of side

Essential Information

The largest subtropical wilderness in the continental USA is easily accessible from Miami. The Glades, which comprise the 80 southernmost miles of Florida, are bound by the Atlantic Ocean to the east and the Gulf of Mexico to the west. The Tamiami Trail (Hwy 41) goes east–west, parallel to the more northern (and less interesting) Alligator Alley (I-75).

paths and canoe creeks for memorable detours. You'll see some of the most quietly exhilarating scenery the park has to offer on this route, and you'll have better access to an interior network of trails for those wanting to push off the beaten track into the buggy, muggy solar plexus of the wetlands. ∎

CLASSIC ROAD TRIPS

The Everglades Tour

The enticing Everglades make South Florida truly unique. This ecological wonderland is the USA's largest subtropical wilderness, flush with endangered and rare species, including its star attraction, the alligator (lots of them). It's not just a wetland, swamp, prairie or grassland – it's all of the above, twisted into a series of soft horizons, panoramic views and sunsets that stretch across your entire field of vision.

Distance 170 miles/274km

Duration 2–3 days

Best Time to Go

December to April is best for both weather and wildlife.

Essential Photo

Alligators lounging in the sun at Shark Valley.

Best for Families

Milkshakes and a petting zoo at Robert Is Here.

❶ Southeastern Everglades

Begin your Everglades adventure at **Ernest Coe Visitor Center** (www.nps.gov/ever; 40001 State Rd 9336), with excellent, museum-quality exhibits and tons of information on park activities. Check ahead for a schedule of ranger-led programs, most of which start 4 miles down at **Royal Palm Visitor**

Center (☎305-242-7237; www.nps.gov/ever/planyourvisit/royal-palm.htm; State Rd 9336; ⏱9am-4:15pm). You'll also find the short **Anhinga Trail** here that offers astounding wildlife-watching opportunities.

Heading further into the park, several trails and scenic viewpoints give you a closer look at the landscape, including **Pa-hay-okee Overlook**, a raised platform that peeks over one of the prettiest bends in the river of grass, and the challenging **Christian Point Trail**, which runs through mangrove forest, prairie and hardwood hammock to the edge of Florida Bay.

The Drive » Continue southwest on SR 9336, which takes you past long fields of marsh prairie, white, skeletal forests of bald cypress and dark clumps of mahogany hammock. The Flamingo Visitor Center is 34 miles south of Royal Palm.

❷ Flamingo

You've come this far, and for your efforts you're rewarded with the opportunity to canoe into the bracken heart of the swamp. Hit the **Flamingo Visitor Center** (www.nps.gov/ever; State Rd 9336) for a map of local canoe trails, such as **Nine Mile Pond**, a 5.2-mile loop that leads you into Florida Bay. You can rent canoes and kayaks at **Flamingo Marina**, and be transported to various trailheads for an additional fee. While you're at the marina, it's worth sticking around to see if any manatees show up. This is also a great spot to see the rare American crocodile.

The Drive » Head back the way you came in; it's the only way out. Six miles past Ernest Coe Visitor Center, go north on Tower Rd. You'll pass the **Robert Is Here** (www.robertishere.com; 19200 SW 344th St, Homestead) fruit stand and then Homestead is just a few miles further up.

❸ Homestead/Florida City

Every good road trip needs a kooky tourist attraction, and thus Homestead – in addition to being a good base of operations for the southeastern portion of the Everglades – humbly offers up the **Coral Castle** (www.coralcastle.com; 28655 S Dixie Hwy), which isn't a castle at all but a monument to both unrequited love and all that is weird and wacky about southern Florida.

In the early 20th century, a Latvian man who had been left at the altar channeled his grief into building a sculpture garden out of more than 1000 tons of coral rock. That he did it by himself, in the dead of night (when it was cooler), using no heavy machinery imbues the place with a sense of mystery. At the very least, it's an impressive feat of engineering.

The Drive » Head 20 miles due north on FL 997/177th Ave until you hit the Tamiami Trail, aka US 41. Shark Valley is 18 miles west. Look for alligators (unless you're driving) in the canal that runs alongside the road.

❹ Shark Valley

Alligators, alligators and more alligators! If that's what you've come to find, you won't be disappointed at **Shark Valley** (www.nps. gov/ever/planyourvisit/svdirections.htm; 36000

SW 8th St). Kick back and enjoy the view during an excellent two-hour **tram tour** (www.sharkvalleytramtours.com) that follows a 15-mile asphalt trail where you'll see copious numbers of alligators in the winter months.

Not only do you get to experience the park from the shady comfort of a breezy tram, but the tour is narrated by knowledgeable park rangers who give a fascinating overview of the Everglades and its inhabitants. Halfway along the trail the tour stops long enough to let you climb a 50ft-high observation tower, an out-of-place concrete structure that offers a dramatic panorama of the park.

The Drive » Exiting the park, turn left onto Tamiami Trail, then immediately turn back off again. The Miccosukee Village is just past the park entrance.

❺ Miccosukee Village

Not so much a quaint little Native American village as it is a handful of commercial

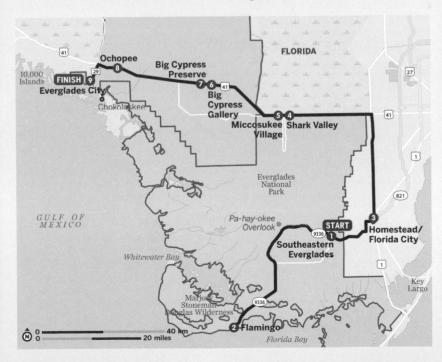

ventures, the Miccosukee Village nonetheless offers insight into Native American life in the Everglades. The centerpiece of the village is the **Miccosukee Indian Museum** (www.miccosukee.com; Mile 70, Hwy 41), just half a mile down the road from Shark Valley.

This informative open-air museum showcases the culture of the Miccosukee via guided tours of traditional homes, a crafts gift store, and dance and music performances. Be aware that the performances include live alligator shows in which a tribal member wrestles with a gator before inviting visitors to have their picture taken while holding one of these prehistoric creatures. You may wish to consider this when deciding whether to visit.

Across the road, catch an **airboat ride** that includes a stop at a Miccosukee camp that's more than 100 years old.

The Drive » Continuing west on Tamiami Trail, you'll pass trees, trees and more trees. After about 20 minutes you'll see Big Cypress Gallery on your left.

❻ Big Cypress Gallery

If you're torn as to the relative beauty of the Everglades, stop by the **Big Cypress Gallery** (https://clydebutcher.com; 52388 Tamiami Trail), featuring the stunning, black-and-white photography of Clyde Butcher. The photographer has been capturing the essence of the Everglades for over 40 years, and there's something about seeing his large-scale prints – some of which are taller than you are – that will make you see the Everglades in a whole new way.

The Drive » The Oasis Visitor Center is on the right, less than a mile west of Big Cypress Gallery.

❼ Big Cypress Preserve

North of the Tamiami Trail you'll find this enormous undeveloped preserve that's integral to the Everglades' ecosystem. Encompassing 1139 sq miles, the preserve is indeed big, so where to start? Orient yourself at the **Oasis Visitor Center** (www. nps.gov/bicy; 52105 Tamiami Trail E). In addition to trail maps you'll find great exhibits for

the kids and an outdoor, water-filled ditch popular with alligators.

Further down Tamiami Trail, but still part of the preserve, you'll find the **Kirby Storter Boardwalk**, a short elevated stroll through a mature cypress dome replete with orchids, bromeliads and the possibility of wildlife that makes you glad it's elevated.

The Drive » Keep going: your next stop is 16 miles west of the Oasis Visitor Center (and 8 miles past Kirby Storter Boardwalk).

❽ Ochopee

In tiny Ochopee, you'll find the **Skunk Ape Research Headquarters** (www.skunkape. info; 40904 Tamiami Trail E), a tongue-in-cheek endeavor dedicated to finding the southeastern USA's version of Bigfoot. The gift shop stocks all your skunk-ape necessities, and there's even a reptile and bird zoo out back run by a true Florida eccentric, the sort of guy who wraps albino pythons around his neck for fun. While you're there, look into **Everglades Adventure Tours** (EAT; www.evergladesadventuretours.com; 40904 Tamiami Trail E), offering some of the best private tours of the Everglades we've found, led by some genuinely funny guys with great local knowledge.

Ochopee is also home to the **Smallest Post Office in the United States**, a comically tiny edifice with very limited hours (you try sitting in there for more than a few hours a day). It's a fun photo op, and a great place to mail a postcard.

The Drive » Just over 4 miles west of the post office, turn left onto CR 29 and go 3 more miles to reach the not-so-booming town of Everglades City.

❾ Everglades City

One of the best ways to experience the serenity of the Everglades is by paddling the network of waterways that skirt the northwest portion of the park. Somehow desolate yet lush, tropical and foreboding, the **10,000 Islands** consist of many (though not 10,000) tiny islands and a mangrove swamp that hugs the southwesternmost border of Florida.

Most islands are fringed by narrow beaches with sugar-white sand, but note that the water is brackish, and very shallow most of the time. It's not Tahiti, but it's fascinating. **The Wilderness Waterway**, a 99-mile path between Everglades City and Flamingo, is the longest canoe trail in the area. Look for canoe rentals and guided boat trips at the **Gulf Coast Visitor Center** (www.nps.gov/ever; 815 Oyster Bar Lane, off Hwy 29, Everglades City).

Top: Post office, Ochopee; Bottom: Kayaking, Everglades

THE SOUTH

In This Chapter

Congaree 58

Great Smoky Mountains 60

Hot Springs 86

Mammoth Cave 96

The South

Mighty mountains, meandering waterways, yawning caves...all are gathered in the South. Here you'll find America's most-visited national park, the Great Smoky Mountains, replete with sparkling waterfalls and foggy peaks to conquer. Meanwhile, Mammoth Caves beckons travelers to stroll, scramble or spelunk through a subterranean wonderland.

More leisurely pursuits await at the piping-hot waters of Hot Springs and Congaree, where days are spent canoeing through high-rise hardwood forests.

Don't Miss

o Drinking in panoramic views on the Charlies Bunion & Kephart Loop (p72)

o Gawping at grottoes in Mammoth Cave (p96)

o Canoeing among cypresses in Congaree (p58)

o Being kissed by mist in Laurel Falls (p67)

o A historic spa experience in Hot Springs (p86)

When to Go

Springtime (April to June) is mild and abloom with flowers. It's a good time to beat the crowds if you don't mind nights that can dip below freezing.

Summer gets steamy, often unpleasantly so. The Smoky Mountains can be frustratingly crowded from June to August but this is prime time for water sports, higher-elevation trails and ranger-led activities. In October, fall foliage is a sight to melt the heart.

The snowy months of December through February draw only hardy, well-prepared souls.

Previous page: Great Smoky Mountains National Park (p60)
SEAN PAVONE/SHUTTERSTOCK ©

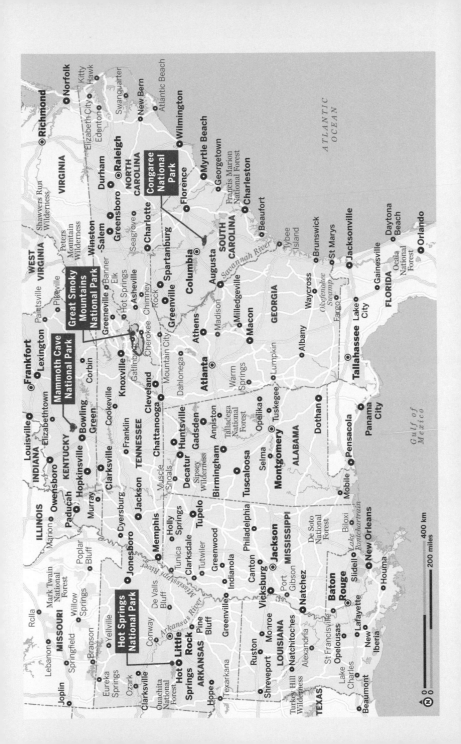

JASON YODER/SHUTTERSTOCK ©

Congaree National Park

The largest old-growth, bottomland hardwood forest in the southeastern US, this floodplain ecosystem has meandering waterways and a sky-high canopy replete with champion trees. The park was established in 1976 and remains an excellent place to canoe and hike, as you occasionally glance skyward at upland pines and bald cypresses.

Great For...

State
South Carolina

Entrance Fee
Free

Area
35 sq miles

Hiking

There are 10 walking trails serving all ages and levels of athleticism, ranging from half a mile to nearly 12 miles.

The popular 2.4-mile **boardwalk**, which begins at the visitor center, takes about an hour to complete. Wheelchairs, strollers and dogs are all welcomed.

The 6.6-mile **Oakridge Trail** is among the best hikes in the state, with its lofty oaks and scenic creeks.

Canoeing & Kayaking

Cedar Creek's ink-black waters wind through 27 miles of wilderness, and canoeing is an ideal way to explore the park, particularly on the seasonal, ranger-led **Wilderness Canoe Tour**.

Another option is to rent a canoe or take a guided tour with Columbia-based **River Runner Outdoor Center** (☏803-771-0353; www.shopriverrunner.com; 905 Gervais St).

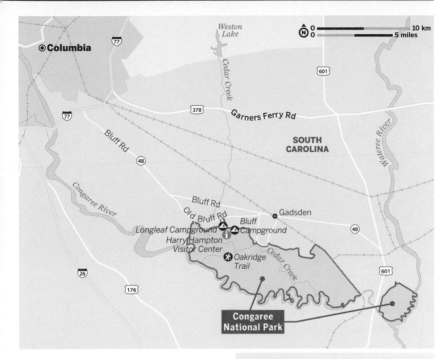

Sleeping & Eating

Tent camping is the only overnight option in Congaree National Park. **Longleaf Campground** (☏877-444-6777; www. recreation.gov; campsites for up to 8/24 people $10/20) is easily accessible by car along the entrance road, and the further-flung **Bluff Campground** (☏877-444-6777; www. recreation.gov; tent sites for up to 8 people $5) requires a mile's hike. Backcountry camping is also available and free; guests must register with the the visitor center.

For those who prefer a bed and walls, Columbia (a 30-minute drive away) has good hotels, including lovely historic inns.■

Essential Information

Harry Hampton Visitor Center (☏803-776-4396; www.nps.gov/cong; 100 National Park Rd, Hopkins; ☉9am-5pm) has an auditorium showing an 18-minute film on the park, a museum and a bookstore selling field guides, snacks, souvenirs and other items.

Mosquito Meter

Be sure to check the 'mosquito meter' at the visitor center so you know what you're getting into. It will let you know on a scale of 1 to 6 how buggy the park will be.

DAVE ALLEN PHOTOGRAPHY/SHUTTERSTOCK ©

Great Smoky Mountains National Park

Part of the vast Appalachian chain, among the oldest mountains on the planet, this is a forested, four-season wonderland. Get back to nature among mist-shrouded peaks, shimmering waterfalls and lush forests in this great American wilderness.

Great For...

State
North Carolina & Tennessee

Entrance Fee
Free

Area
816 sq miles

Great Smoky Mountains National Park straddles the North Carolina and Tennessee border, which runs diagonally through the heart of the park, shadowed by the Appalachian Trail.

Cades Cove

In Appalachian parlance, a cove means a valley, but Cades Cove is far more than that. Many consider this special place to be a national treasure, thanks to its poignant cultural legacy, telling pioneer architecture and plentiful wildlife. Then there's the landscape itself: lush green fields enveloped by an unbroken expanse of mountains. It's no wonder so many families return year after year. The best wildlife viewing is in the very early morning and late afternoon.

Because of bumper-to-bumper traffic during peak season, it can take five hours to drive the 11-mile one-way loop

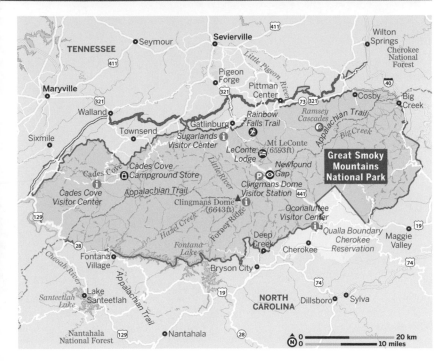

road – longer than it would take to walk! The loop road is open to car traffic from dawn to dusk, except on Wednesdays and Saturdays from early May through late September, when bicycles and hikers rule the road until 10am. Pick up the self-guiding *Cades Cove Tour* booklet ($1) from any visitor center.

Mt LeConte

The park's third-highest peak and one of its most familiar sights, Mt LeConte (6593ft) is visible from practically every viewpoint. The only way to the top is on foot. It is accessible on five trails, which range from 5 to 8.9 miles in length.

Reaching the summit (located 0.2 miles above the lodge) is a challenging goal, and it's well worth the effort. Aside from great views, you can stop in the office and lounge at **LeConte Lodge** to check out photos of cabin life dating back to the 1930s and browse the small shop.

Hiking Trails

Even if you're only here for a short visit, be sure to include at least one hike in your itinerary. Trails range from flat, easy and short paths to longer, more strenuous endeavors.

The trail to **Ramsey Cascades** travels through old-growth forest dotted with massive tulip trees to one spectacular waterfall. The hike's start is deceptively easy, along a wide, packed trail but you'll need to work hard to make it all the way – it's tough going, with an elevation gain of 2280ft. Also a slog is the **Rainbow Falls Trail**, which involves ascending 1600ft in a scant 2.7 miles. But oh, is it worth it when you see misty Rainbow Falls, one of the park's prettiest and most delicate waterfalls.

Near the start of the Roaring Fork Motor Nature Trail, the **Baskins Creek Trail** is a fascinating 5.6-mile (round-trip) out-and-back hike, drawing a fraction of the

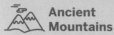

Ancient Mountains

The story of the Smoky Mountains began in primordial times when clashing supersized continents created a chain of mountains that are today among the oldest on the planet. Humans have also left their mark on these ancient Appalachian landscapes. Nomadic tribes were the first to the area, followed by early settlers. In the 1900s lumber companies arrived, nearly wiping out the forests. Luckily, in the 1920s a few visionary locals fought for the park's creation, which finally became a reality in 1934.

On November 23, 2016 tragedy struck Great Smoky Mountains National Park when fire was reported on Chimney Tops, one of the park's most popular trails. The combination of exceptional drought conditions, low humidity and wind gusts that topped 80 miles an hour caused the fire to spread quickly in what would soon become the the deadliest wildfire in the eastern USA since the Great Fires of 1947. There were 14 deaths, 175 injuries, more than 2400 structures damaged or destroyed, and the forced evacuation of 14,000 residents.

Top: Baskins Creek Trail; Bottom right: Ramsey
Cascades; Bottom left: LeConte Lodge

number of visitors to more popular nearby
sites. Along the way, you'll spy white vein
quartz, see fire-blackened tree trunks
from the 2016 fires and make a few creek
crossings.

Cycling

Bicycles are welcome on most park roads,
with the exception of the Roaring Fork
Motor Nature Trail. However, it is important
that you choose your road wisely. Because
of steep terrain, narrow byways and heavy
car traffic, many park roads are not well
suited to safe or enjoyable riding. Great
Smoky has no mountain-biking trails.
Bicycles are allowed only on the Gatlinburg
Trail, the Oconaluftee River Trail and the
Lower Deep Creek Trail. They are prohibited on all other park trails.

By far the best place for a carefree
cycling tour is Cades Cove, particularly
when the road is closed to cars (Wednes-
day and Sunday before 10am from
mid-May to late September). In summer
and fall, rent cycles from **Cades Cove
Campground Store** (🕿865-448-9034; www.
cadescovetrading.com; 10035 Campground Dr;
⊗9am-9pm late May-Oct, to 5pm Mar-May, Nov
& late Dec).

Rafting

Many winding creeks and crystal-clear
streams rushing through the Smokies find
their way into the Big Pigeon River. When
they converge, they create a fantastic setting for **white-water adventures** (🕿800-
776-7238; www.raftinginthesmokies.com; rafting
trip $35-42) on churning rapids amid a
gorgeous forest backdrop. Families with
small kids can enjoy a peaceful paddle on
the Lower Pigeon, while those seeking a bit
more adventure should opt for the Upper
Pigeon with its class III and IV rapids. It all
makes for a fun day's outing with some of
the best rafting in the southeast.

Horseback Riding

A staggering – or should we say galloping – 550 miles of the park's hiking trails are open to horses and their humans. Assuming you're not towing your own horse, sign on for a trail ride at one of the park's three stables (www.nps.gov/grsm/planyourvisit/horseriding.htm), all open between mid-March and mid-November. It's best to call ahead to make reservations.

One-hour trail rides cost about $35 per person. Those who want a bit more saddle time can sign up for longer rides, ranging from 2½ to four hours. Unfortunately, the park no longer offers overnight trips.

Top left: Alum Cave Bluffs; Top right: Rainbow Falls; Bottom: Cades Cove

TOP LEFT: THERON STRIPLING III/SHUTTERSTOCK © TOP RIGHT: KURDISTAN/SHUTTERSTOCK ©

Plan Your Trip

The park is open year-round, but summer and fall are the most popular seasons. Some facilities are closed late fall through early spring, and roads may be closed in winter due to inclement weather.

Newfound Gap Rd/Hwy 441 is the only thoroughfare that crosses Great Smoky Mountains National Park, winding through the mountains from Gatlinburg, TN, to the town of Cherokee, NC, passing en route the busy Oconaluftee Visitor Center in the park's southeast.

Hike Alum Cave Bluffs

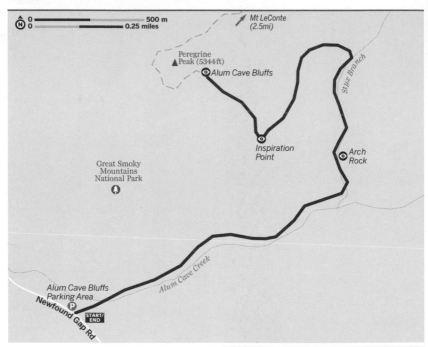

Try to be on the trail before 9am to avoid crowds. From the trailhead along Newfound Gap Rd, you quickly leave the sounds of traffic behind as you cross a stout bridge over a gurgling mountain stream and enter a wilderness of rosebay rhododendrons and thick ferns, with American beech and yellow birch trees soaring overhead.

Soon you'll be following along the rushing waters of **Alum Cave Creek**. Enjoy this fairly flat, scenic stretch as the climbing begins after Mile 1.1.

At that point you'll cross the **Styx Branch**. From here it's about 600yd to **Arch Rock**, a picturesque natural tunnel, which you'll pass through along carved stone steps leading up the steep slope.

The tough ascent continues, leading past old-growth hardwoods as it winds up **Peregrine Peak**. Around Mile 1.8 you'll reach a heath bald where the views begin to open up. A bit further (around Mile 2), you'll reach the aptly named **Inspiration Point**, offering

Duration 2½–3½ hours round-trip

Distance 4.6 miles

Difficulty Hard

Elevation Change 2200ft

Start & Finish Alum Cave Bluffs parking area

even more impressive views of the forested valley below. Stop here to catch your breath before pressing on the final 600yd to **Alum Cave Bluffs**. Despite the name, this is not a cave but rather an 80ft-high concave cliff.

Though most people turn around here, you can press on to **Mt LeConte**, another 2.7 miles uphill, if you still have plenty of energy left. The terrain on this stretch is particularly challenging, as the trail passes over narrow rock ledges – steel cables bolted into the mountain provide useful handholds. Otherwise, it's an easy downhill descent back to your starting point.

Hike Laurel Falls

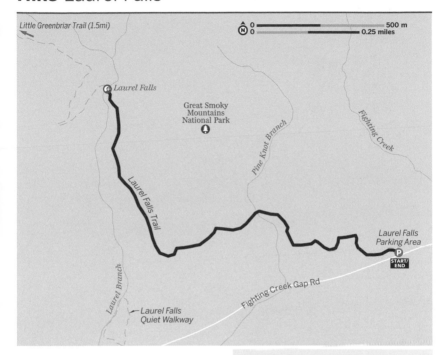

This is one of the most popular waterfall trails in the park. Come very early or late in the day to beat the worst of the crowds. The park service has paved the entire length of the trail. Although it's smooth going, the trail is a little too steep for strollers and wheelchairs, though we have spotted both on the trail.

From the parking area, the trail starts out with a short steep section, then continues along a steady uphill rise past small shrub-like mountain laurels (which turn the hills pink and white in early summer) and stands of rhododendrons. Continuing uphill, you'll soon pass pines, maples and dogwoods before the view opens up to your left and reveals a fine outlook over the valley. Further ahead, you'll pass rocks on your left, which the Civilian Conservation Corps had to partially blast their way through to create the trail back in the 1930s.

The trail continues uphill, at times growing narrower. If in a group, you'll want

Duration 1½–2 hours round trip
Distance 2.6 miles
Difficulty Easy–moderate
Elevation Change 310ft
Start & Finish Laurel Falls parking area

to go single file, and watch your step in cold weather as it can be icy (a sign reminds hikers that falls have resulted in deaths here).

At Mile 1.3 you have arrived. Powered by annual rainfall of 55in, the 75ft-high waterfall is a refreshing sight, though it's nearly always packed. After taking in the view, you can either make the return descent or leave the crowds behind and continue along the trail, which intersects with the Little Greenbrier Trail at Mile 3.1.

Look for the trailhead (and many, many cars parked along the road) on the north side of Fighting Creek Gap Rd, about 3.8 miles west of the Sugarlands Visitor Center.

Drive Newfound Gap Road

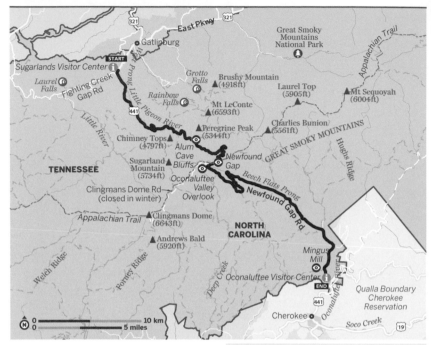

The park's main artery, Newfound Gap Rd/ Hwy 441, begins just outside Gatlinburg and heads 33 winding miles to Cherokee, NC, passing many turnouts, picnic areas, nature trails and overlooks along the way.

Between Mile 5.6 and Mile 7.1, you'll have several opportunities to pull over and admire one of the park's best-known geologic features, **Chimney Tops**. The Cherokee called these twin stony outcroppings high on the ridge 'Duniskwalgunyi' as they resembled a pair of antlers, while white settlers characterized them as a pair of stone chimneys.

The trailhead and parking area for one of the park's most popular hikes, **Alum Cave Bluffs**, is at Mile 8.8. At Mile 12.2 you'll know you've entered the cooler upper elevations of the Smokies as you come to the spruce fir forest that dominates the high mountain slopes.

At **Newfound Gap** travelers pass from Tennessee into North Carolina and the

Duration 1–3 hours

Distance 33 miles

Start Sugarlands Visitor Center

Finish Oconaluftee Visitor Center

Appalachian Trail crosses the road. Straddling the state line is the Rockefeller Memorial, marking the spot where Franklin D Roosevelt formally dedicated the park in 1940.

The turnoff for Clingmans Dome Rd is at Mile 13.4. Shortly thereafter, at Mile 13.9, is a large parking area for the impressive **Oconaluftee Valley Overlook**.

At Mile 28.7, **Mingus Mill** still grinds corn into meal just as it has done for more than a century. The mill operates from early spring through fall, though visitors are welcome any time. It's just a half-mile from the Oconaluftee Visitor Center (p70), signaling the end of the driving tour.

Drive Roaring Forks Motor Nature Trail

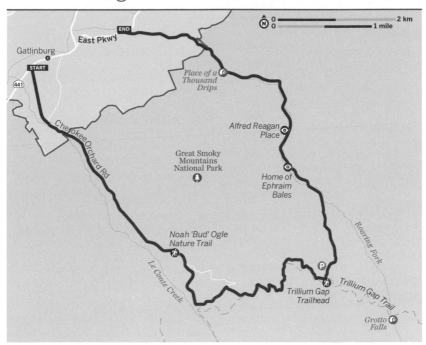

If you happen to be in the park during a thunderstorm, don't let it ruin your day – this quick drive is at its best after a particularly hard rain. Keep in mind: the Roaring Trail is closed in winter – it's accessible only from late April to November.

From Hwy 441 in Gatlinburg, turn onto Airport Rd, which becomes Cherokee Orchard Rd. The Roaring Fork Motor Nature Trail begins 3 miles later.

The first stop on Cherokee Orchard Rd is the **Noah 'Bud' Ogle Nature Trail**, providing an enjoyable jaunt into a mountain farmstead with a streamside tub mill (for grinding the family corn) and an ingenious wooden-flume plumbing apparatus.

From the Trillium Gap Trailhead the delicate **Grotto Falls** can be reached via a short hike through a virgin hemlock forest.

Roaring Fork Rd is a narrow, twisting road that follows **Roaring Fork**, one of the park's most tempestuous and beautiful streams. It passes through an impressive stand of

Duration 1–2 hours

Distance 8.5 miles

Start Historic Nature Trail Rd, Gatlinburg

Finish Roaring Fork Rd, Gatlinburg

old-growth eastern hemlocks, some of which reach heights of more than 100ft and have trunks stretching as much as 5ft across.

Of considerable historical interest is the hardscrabble cabin at the **Home of Ephraim Bales** and also the more comfortable 'saddlebag' house at the **Alfred Reagan Place** (painted with 'all three colors that Sears and Roebuck had'). Reagan was a jack-of-all-trades who served his community as a carpenter, blacksmith and storekeeper.

A wet-weather waterfall called **Place of a Thousand Drips** provides a wonderful conclusion to your explorations before returning to Gatlinburg.

Essential Information

Sleeping

The only place where you can get a room is **LeConte Lodge** (☎865-429-5704; www.lecontelodge.com; cabins incl breakfast & dinner adult $148, child 4-12yr $85; ⊗mid-Mar–mid-Nov) and you have to hike to the top of a mountain to enjoy the privilege. Gatlinburg has the most sleeping options of any gateway town, though prices are high. Nearby Pigeon Forge, 10 miles north of Sugarlands Visitor Center, and Sevierville, 17 miles north, have cheaper options.

Camping

The National Park Service (NPS) maintains developed campgrounds at nine locations in the park (a 10th remains closed indefinitely). Each campground has restrooms with cold running water and flush toilets, but there are no showers or electrical or water hookups in the park (though some campgrounds do have electricity for emergency situations). Many sites can be reserved in advance, and several campgrounds (Cataloochee, Abrams Creek, Big Creek and Balsam Mountain) require advance reservations. Reserve through www.recreation.gov.

Plan ahead in the busy summer season. Cades Cove and Smokemont campgrounds are open year-round; others are open March to October.

Backcountry camping is only chargeable up to five nights ($4 per night; after that, it's free). A permit is required. You can make reservations online at http://smokiespermits.nps.gov, and get permits at the ranger stations or visitor centers.

Eating

Bring a cooler and load up on groceries. There are lovely spots for a picnic, and it's a waste of time driving out of the park to lunch spots during the day.

Find vending machines at Sugarlands Visitor Center and some meager offerings sold at the Cades Cove Campground store. If you make the hike up to LeConte Lodge, you can purchase cookies, drinks and sack lunches.

Information

Cades Cove Visitor Center (☎865-436-7318; www.nps.gov/grsm; ⊗9am-7pm Apr-Aug, closes earlier Sep-Mar) Halfway up Cades Cove Loop Rd, 24 miles off Hwy 441 from the Gatlinburg entrance.

Clingmans Dome Visitor Station (☎865-436-1200; ⊗10am-6pm Apr-Oct, 9:30am-5pm Nov) Small, very busy center at the start of the paved path up to the Clingmans Dome lookout.

Oconaluftee Visitor Center (☎828-497-1904; www.nps.gov/grsm; ⊗8am-7pm Jun-Aug, to 6pm Apr, May, Sep & Oct, to 4:30pm Nov-Mar; 🖘) ⚑ At the park's southern entrance near Cherokee in North Carolina.

Sugarlands Visitor Center (☎865-436-1291; www.nps.gov/grsm; ⊗8am-7:30pm Jun-Aug, hours vary Sep-May; 🖘) At the park's northern entrance near Gatlinburg.

Park Policies & Regulations

Visitors are required to stay at least 50yd from any wildlife – this is especially true of elk. Feeding wildlife is prohibited (with a fine of up to $5000).

Accessible Travel

The park has one excellent trail that is accessible: the smooth, half-mile Sugarlands Valley Nature Trail. Other places worth exploring include historic sites in Cades Cove, which has hard-packed gravel paths running around the area. Buildings can be viewed only from the exterior, though the Cable Mill and the Becky Cable House are both accessible via a ramp.

Getting There & Around

The closest airports to the national park are McGhee Tyson Airport near Knoxville (40 miles northwest of the Sugarlands Visitor Center) and Asheville Regional Airport, 58 miles east of the Oconaluftee Visitor Center.

There's no public transportation to the park. There's a wide variety of car-rental outfits at each of the airports.

Top left: Alfred Reagan Place; Top right: Roaring Fork Creek; Bottom: Newfound Gap Road

CLASSIC HIKES

Charlies Bunion & Kephart Loop

The rocky outcropping known as Charlies Bunion offers one of the most memorable panoramas in the park. Most visitors do Charlies Bunion as an out-and-back day hike (8 miles return), but you can leave the day-trippers behind and overnight in a lush valley near the Kephart Prong.

Distance 14 miles

Duration 2 days

Difficulty Moderate

Start & Finish Newfound Gap

Elevation Change 4185ft

Nearest Town/Junction Gatlinburg

DAY 1: Newfound Gap to Kephart Prong (4 hours, 8.5 miles)

The hike starts near the **Rockefeller Memorial**, which straddles two states at Newfound Gap, around 13 miles south of the Sugarlands Visitor Center. Check out the views into Tennessee and North Carolina, then find the sign indicating the Appalachian Trail just below. Hit the trail early if you want the scenery to yourself.

The first 2 miles of the hike follow a fairly steady elevation gain along cool, mixed forest before passing through Fraser fir forest, the bare limbs of the trees evidence of the balsam woolly adelgid wreaking havoc. You'll also see plenty of

wildflowers in spring and blackberries in late summer.

Around Mile 1.7, you'll pass the junction with the Sweat Heifer Creek Trail, which you'll be going up the next day. A little further along, around Mile 2.7, you'll pass the turnoff to the Boulevard Trail, which leads up to Mt LeConte. A little further along, the Icewater Spring shelter is a popular overnight stop for through hikers. The piped spring just beyond does indeed have ice-cold water, though as elsewhere in the park, you'll need to treat it before drinking. From here the path descends through a cool spruce and fir forest before leveling out amid secondary forest of American beech and yellow birch. After a short ascent, you'll see the big rock face just ahead. Then at Mile 4.0, a well-weathered signpost announces your arrival at **Charlies Bunion**.

As you take the narrow spur out to the overlook, keep in mind that careless travelers have fallen to their death out on the rocks, so it's best not to scramble around on these ledges. The curious name, incidentally, comes from Horace Kephart, who was out exploring this section of the Smokies in 1929 with his friend Charlie Connor and photographer George Masa. After spotting the bulbous rock face, he paid homage to his hiking companion (or at least his companion's foot ailment), saying, jovially, that it looked just like Charlie's bunion. Somehow the farcical name stuck – it helped that Kephart was later involved in choosing place names within the park boundaries. If you haven't eaten already, this is a fine place for a long break. With dizzying 1000ft drop-offs, the sweeping panorama spreads from Mt LeConte eastward to the the jagged peaks of the Sawteeth Range.

From Charlies Bunion, you'll continue along the Appalachian Trail for another half-mile before making the right (southward) turn onto the Dry Sluice Gap Trail. You'll likely have this quiet, little-used track all to yourself as you descend through stands of Catawba rhododendrons – at times so thick, they form an enclosed Gothic arch overhead. Around Mile 5.8, you'll see the signpost for the Grassy Branch Trail leading off to your right. Take this trail, which keeps descending. You'll pass wind-whipped oak and birch trees, and cross a few small streams, including an offshoot of the Icewater Spring that you traversed far above.

After the long, steady descent, you'll soon hear the rush of the **Kephart Prong**. Then around Mile 8.4, you'll reach a forest of rich secondary growth and arrive at the **Kephart Shelter**. After dropping your pack (and hoisting up your food items with the bear-proof cable system), you can explore a bit of this former lumber site. Try

to get plenty of rest, because you'll have lots of climbing on day two.

DAY 2: Sweat Heifer Creek Trail to Newfound Gap (2.5 hours, 5.5 miles, 2500ft ascent)

The day begins along the Sweat Heifer Creek Trail, which starts a few paces from the shelter. Cross a log bridge over the rushing stream and mossy boulders, then make the slow, steady ascent. Plan a rest stop around Mile 1.6 (from the shelter), beside the cooling multi-stage falls of **Sweat Heifer Cascades**. At Mile 3.8 you'll meet back up with the Appalachian Trail. Turn left and continue another 1.7 miles to return to your original starting point. ∎

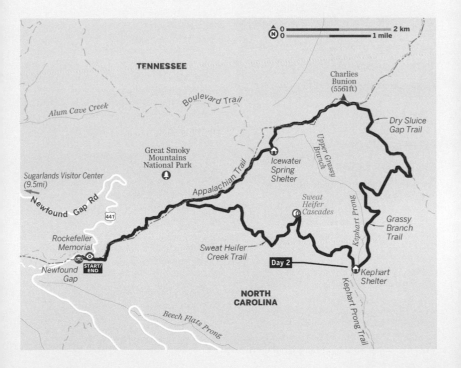

CLASSIC ROAD TRIPS

Blue Ridge Parkway Tour

The Blue Ridge Parkway is an NPS-designated national parkway that winds for 469 sumptuous miles from Virginia's Shenandoah National Park to the Great Smoky Mountains. As it carves through a rugged landscape of craggy peaks, crashing waterfalls and thick forests, each languid curve unveils another panorama of multihued trees and mist-shrouded mountains, with tantalizing viewpoints encouraging frequent stops. No billboards spoil the views, and there's seldom even a sign of human presence.

Distance 210 miles/338km

Duration 5 days

Best Time to Go
May to October for leafy trees and seasonal attractions.

Essential Photo
The mile-high suspension bridge at Grandfather Mountain.

Best for Families
Enjoy a steam-train ride, gem mining, easy hiking and old-fashioned candy.

❶ Valle Crucis
How do you start a road trip through the mountains? With a good night's sleep and all the right gear, of course. You'll find both in Valle Crucis, a bucolic village 8 miles west of Boone. After slumbering beneath sumptuous linens at the 200-year-old **Mast Farm Inn** (www.themastfarminn.com; 2543 Broadstone Rd), ease into the day sipping coffee in a rocking chair on the former farmhouse's front porch.

Down the road lies the **Original Mast General Store** (www.mastgeneralstore.com; 3565 Hwy 194 S). The first of the many Mast general stores that dot the High Country, this rambling clapboard building still sells many of the same products that it did back in 1883. As well as bacon, axes and hard candy, though, you'll now find hiking shoes, lava lamps and French country hand towels.

The store's **annex**, just south along Hwy 194, sells outdoor apparel and hiking gear.

The Drive ❯❯ Drive southeast on Hwy 194, also known as Broadstone Rd, through 3 miles of rural splendor, then turn left at Hwy 105.

❷ Boone
If you're traveling with kids or are a wannabe prospector yourself, stop at **Foggy Mountain Gem Mine** (www.foggymountain gems.com; 4416 Hwy 105 S) to pan for semi-precious stones. Several gem-mining spots are located in these parts, but the graduate gemologists here take their craft a bit more seriously. Rough stones are sold by the bucketload, which you sift in a flume line. For additional fees, they'll cut and mount your favorite finds.

In downtown Boone, the bustling home of Appalachian State, you'll find quirky shopping and dining along **King St**, where **Melanie's Food Fantasy** (www.melaniesfood fantasy.com; 664 W King St) is a good option for a hearty breakfast or tasty lunch. Keep an eye out for the bronze **statue** (642 W King St) of bluegrass legend Doc Watson, born nearby in 1923 and depicted strumming a Gallagher guitar on a street corner.

The Drive ❯❯ From King St, turn onto Hwy 321 just past the Dan'l Boone Inn restaurant. Drive 4 miles then turn right at the theme park.

❸ Blowing Rock

The parkway runs just above the village of Blowing Rock, which sits at an elevation of 4000ft. On a cloudy morning, drive south on Hwy 321 to the top of the mountain to check out the cloud-capped views of surrounding peaks. The eastern continental divide runs through the bar at the **Green Park Inn** (www.greenparkinn.com; 9239 Valley Blvd), a grand white-clapboard hotel that opened in 1891. Author Margaret Mitchell stayed here while writing *Gone with the Wind*. For a memorable meal in a century-old lodge, call in at **Bistro Roca** (www.bistro roca.com; 143 Wonderland Trail).

Riding the **Tweetsie Railroad** (www.tweet sie.com; 300 Tweetsie Railroad Lane), a 1917 coal-fired steam locomotive that chugs on a 3-mile loop, is a rite of passage for every North Carolina child. It's the centerpiece of a theme park where Appalachian culture meets the Wild West, with midway rides, fudge shops and family-friendly shows to round out the fun.

The Drive » The entrance to the Blue Ridge Parkway is in Blowing Rock, 2.3 miles south of the Tweetsie Railroad. Once on the parkway, drive south 2 miles.

❹ Moses H Cone Memorial Park

Hikers and equestrians share 25 miles of carriage roads on the former estate of Moses H Cone, a philanthropist and conservationist who made his fortune in denim. Moses built a Colonial Revival mansion, Flat Top Manor, in 1901, which was given, along with the grounds, to the National Park Service in the 1950s. Directly accessible from the parkway at Mile 294, it now holds both a museum and the **Parkway Craft Center** (www.southernhighlandguild.org; Mile 294), where the Southern Highland Craft Guild sells superb Appalachian crafts at reasonable prices.

The Drive » Head south on the park-way, passing split rail fences, stone walls,

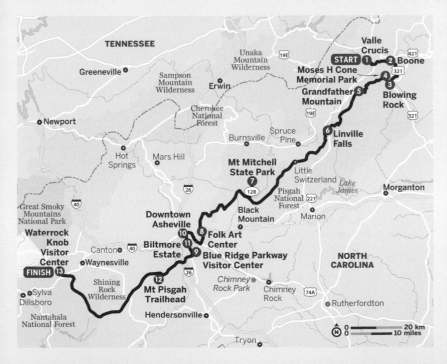

Blue Ridge Parkway Trip Planner

o Driving the parkway is not so much a way to get from A to B – don't expect to get anywhere fast – as an experience to relish.

o The maximum speed limit is 45mph.

o Long stretches of the parkway close in winter, and may not reopen until March, while many visitor centers and campgrounds remain closed until May. Check the park-service website (www.nps.gov/blri) for more information.

o The North Carolina section of the parkway starts at Mile 216.9, between the Blue Ridge Mountain Center in Virginia and Cumberland Knob in North Carolina.

o There are 26 tunnels on the park-way in North Carolina, as opposed to just one in Virginia. Watch for signs to turn on your headlights.

o For more help with trip planning, check the websites of the Blue Ridge Parkway Association (www. blueridgeparkway.org) and the Blue Ridge National Heritage Area (www. blueridgeheritage.com).

streams and meadows. Just south of Mile 304, the parkway curves across the Linn Cove Viaduct, which, because of the fragility of the terrain, was the final section of the parkway to be completed, in 1987. Exit onto Hwy 221 at Mile 305, and drive 1 mile south.

❺ Grandfather Mountain

The highest of the Blue Ridge Mountains, **Grandfather Mountain** (www.grandfather. com; 2050 Blowing Rock Hwy, Linville) looms north of the parkway 20 miles southwest of Blowing Rock. As a visitor destination, it's famous as the location of the Mile High Swinging Bridge, the focus of a privately owned attraction that also includes hiking trails plus a small museum and wildlife reserve. Don't let a fear of heights scare you

away. Though the bridge is a mile above sea level, and on gusty days you can hear its steel girders 'sing,' it spans a less fearsome chasm that's just 80ft deep.

Much of Grandfather Mountain – including its loftiest summit, Calloway Peak (5946ft), a strenuous 2.4-mile hike from the swinging bridge – is a Unesco Biosphere Reserve belonging to Grand-father Mountain State Park (www.ncparks. gov). Its 12 miles of wilderness hiking trails can also be accessed for free at Mile 300 on the parkway.

The Drive » Follow the parkway south and turn left just past Mile 316 to reach Linville Falls.

❻ Linville Falls

If you only have time for a single parkway hike, an hour-long sojourn at spectacular **Linville Falls** (www.nps.gov/blri; Mile 316, Blue Ridge Pkwy, Linville) makes a great option. Cross the Linville River from the parking lot, and head along Erwin's View Trail. This moderate 1.6-mile round trip offers great close-up views of the river as it sweeps over two separate falls, before you climb a wooded hillside to enjoy magnificent long-range panoramas in two directions. One looks back to the falls, the other faces downstream, where the river crashes a further 2000ft through a rocky gorge. Swimming is forbidden at the falls.

The Drive » Drive south on the parkway and turn right, south of Mile 355, onto NC 128. Follow NC 128 into the park.

❼ Mt Mitchell State Park

Be warned: a major decision awaits visitors to North Carolina's first-ever **state park** (www.ncparks.gov; 2388 Hwy 128). Will you drive up Mt Mitchell, at 6684ft the highest peak east of the Mississippi, or will you hike to the top? Make your mind up at the park office, which sits beside a steep 2.2-mile summit trail that typically takes around 1½ hours one way.

Once up there, you'll see the grave of University of North Carolina professor

Elisha Mitchell. He came here in 1857 to prove his previous estimate of the mountain's height, only to fall from a waterfall and die. A circular ramp leads to dramatic views over and beyond the surrounding Black Mountains.

The Drive » Return to the parkway and drive south to Mile 382. Look out for blooming rhododendrons during the last two weeks of June.

❽ Folk Art Center

Part gallery, part store, and wholly dedicated to Southern craftsmanship, the superb **Folk Art Center** (www.southern highlandguild.org; Mile 382, Blue Ridge Pkwy) is 6 miles east of downtown Asheville. The handcrafted Appalachian chairs that hang above its lobby make an impressive appetizer for the permanent collection of the Southern Highland Craft Guild, a treasury

of pottery, baskets, quilts and woodcarvings that's displayed on the 2nd floor. There are daily demonstrations by experts, and the Allanstand Craft Shop on the 1st floor sells high-quality traditional crafts.

The Drive » Turn right onto the parkway and drive south. Cross the Swannanoa River and I-40, then continue to Mile 384.

❾ Blue Ridge Parkway Visitor Center

At the Blue Ridge Parkway's helpful Asheville-area **visitor center** (www.nps. gov/blri; Mile 384), you can sit back and let the scenery come to you, courtesy of a big-screen movie that captures the beauty and wonder of 'America's favorite journey.' Park rangers at the front desk gladly advise on parkway hiking trails, and sliding the digital panel across the amazing 'I-Wall'

MARGARET.WIKTOR/SHUTTERSTOCK ©

Grandfather Mountain State Park

Bluegrass & Mountain Music

For locally grown fiddle-and-banjo music, grab your dance partner and head deep into the hills of the High Country. Regional shows and music jams are listed on the Blue Ridge Music Trails (www.blueridgemusicnc.com) and Blue Ridge National Heritage Area (www.blueridgeheritage.com) websites.

Here are three to get you started:

Mountain Home Music Concert Series (www.mountainhomemusic.com) Spring through fall, enjoy shows by Appalachian musicians in Boone on scheduled Saturday nights.

Isis Music Hall (www.isisasheville.com) Local bluegrass greats pop in at this Asheville institution's regular Tuesday-night session.

Historic Orchard at Altapass (www.altapassorchard.org) On weekends in May through October, settle in for an afternoon of music at Little Switzerland, Mile 328.

map brings up details of regional sites and activities. A separate desk is stocked with brochures and coupons for Asheville's attractions.

The Drive » Drive north, backtracking over the interstate and river, and exit at Tunnel Rd, which is Hwy 70. Drive west to Hwy 240, and follow it west to the exits for downtown Asheville.

🔟 Downtown Asheville

The undisputed 'capital' of the North Carolina mountains, Asheville is both a major tourist destination and one of the coolest small cities in the South. Home to an invigorating mix of hipsters, hippies and hikers, and offering easy access to outdoor adventures of all kinds, it's also a rare liberal enclave in the conservative countryside.

Strolling between downtown's historic art-deco buildings, you'll encounter literary pilgrims celebrating the city's angsty

famous son – and author of *Look Homeward, Angel* – at the **Thomas Wolfe Memorial** (www.wolfememorial.com; 52 N Market St); nostalgic gamers flipping the flippers at the **Pinball Museum** (https://pinball.ashevillepinball.com; 1 Battle Sq); left-leaning intellectuals browsing at **Malaprop's Bookstore & Cafe** (www.malaprops.com; 55 Haywood St); and design connoisseurs shopping for crafts in **Horse & Hero** (www.facebook.com/horseandhero; 14 Patton Ave).

Head down the adjoining South Slope to find specialist microbreweries, such as spooky **Burial** (www.burialbeer.com; 40 Collier Ave), which have earned Asheville the nickname 'Beer City,' or hit the River Arts District to enjoy barbecue emporium **12 Bones** (www.12bones.com; 5 Foundy St). Budget travelers looking to stay in Asheville should head for downtown's excellent **Sweet Peas Hostel** (www.sweetpeashostel.com; 23 Rankin Ave).

The Drive » Follow Asheland Ave, which becomes McDowell St, south. After crossing the Swannanoa River, the entrance to the Biltmore Estate is on the right.

⓫ Biltmore Estate

The destination that put Asheville on the map, **Biltmore House** (www.biltmore.com; 1 Approach Rd), is the largest privately owned home in the US. Completed in 1895 for shipping and railroad heir George Washington Vanderbilt II, it was modeled after three châteaux that he'd seen in France's Loire Valley, and still belongs to his descendants. It's extraordinarily expensive to visit, but there's a lot to see; allow several hours to explore the entire 8000-acre Biltmore Estate. Self-guided tours of the house itself take in 39 points of interest.

To hear the full story, pay extra for an audio tour, or take the behind-the-scenes Backstairs Tour or the more architecturally focused Rooftop Tour. A 5-mile drive through the manicured estate, which also holds several cafes and two top-end hotels, leads to the winery and dairy farm in Antler Hill Village.

The Drive » Exit the grounds, then turn right onto Hwy 25 and continue for almost 3.5 miles to the parkway, and drive south.

⑫ Mt Pisgah Trailhead

To enjoy an hour or two of hiking that culminates in a panoramic view, pull into the parking lot beside the **Mt Pisgah** trailhead, just beyond Mile 407. The 1.6-mile trail (one way) climbs to the mountain's 5721ft summit, topped by a lofty TV tower. The going gets steep and rocky in its final stretches, but you'll be rewarded with views of the French Broad River Valley as well as **Cold Mountain**, made famous by Charles Frazier's eponymous novel. One mile south you'll find a campground, a general store, a restaurant and an inn.

The Drive » The drive south passes the Graveyard Fields Overlook, where short trails lead to scenic waterfalls. From the 6047ft Richland Balsam Overlook at Mile 431.4 – the highest point on the parkway – continue south for another 20 miles.

⑬ Waterrock Knob Visitor Center

This trip ends at the Waterrock Knob Visitor Center (Mile 451.2), which sits at an elevation of nearly 6000ft. With a four-state view, this scenic spot is a great place to see where you've been and to assess what lies ahead. Helpful signs identify the mountains along the far horizon.

Biltmore Estate

CLASSIC ROAD TRIPS

Appalachian Trail

Originally the idea of one man, Benton MacKaye, as an antidote to the busy, urban lifestyle of the East Coast in the 1920s, the Appalachian Trail (known as the AT) was completed in 1937. Today it is managed by the National Park Service, US Forest Service, Appalachian Trail Conservancy and numerous state agencies, with assistance from thousands of volunteers. The entire route is marked by a series of 2in x 6in white blazes, and is for foot traffic only. Our road trip will allow you to experience the trail with a minimum of suffering.

Distance 343 miles/552km

Duration 5–7 days

Best Time to Go
From April to October the snow has melted, or hasn't yet begun to fall.

Essential Photo
Max Patch Mountain offers signature views of the lower portion of the AT.

Best for Outdoors
The AT is the original long-distance hiking trail.

❶ Amicalola Falls State Park
There is no better way to get a feel for the grandeur of the Appalachian Trail than at its Georgian gateway, **Amicalola Falls State Park** (www.amicalolafallslodge.com/ga-state-park; 418 Amicalola Falls State Park Rd, Dawsonville). Amicalola, a Cherokee word meaning 'tumbling waters,' is an appropriate name for these 729ft falls – the tallest cascade east of the Mississippi River. The park offers more than 12 miles of hiking trails, including the 8.5 mile **Approach Trail**, past the falls to Springer Mountain, where the Appalachian Trail officially begins.

Get set up with maps and local hiking tips at the **Amicalola Falls State Park Visitors Center** (www.amicalolafallslodge.com/ga-state-park; 418 Amicalola Falls State Park Rd, Dawsonville), which also offers exhibits and a gift shop.

The Drive » Thru-hikers can trek here from Amicalola Falls State Park, but if the 604-step staircase freaks you out, take GA 52E to Winding Stair Gap Rd and you'll find some nice views of Springer Mountain.

❷ Springer Mountain
The Appalachian Trail officially starts on top of this mountain, marked with a plaque: 'A footpath for those who seek fellowship with the wilderness.'

Most thru-hikers (or '2000 milers,' as those who walk the AT in a single journey are known) usually start here, at the Georgia terminus (about two hours north of Atlanta), in the late spring, and finish five to seven months later on Mt Katahdin in Maine, 2175 miles to the north. About 800 registered hikers complete the journey each year, about a quarter of those who set out. Altogether, only about 20,000 brave and hearty trekkers have ever completed the journey. A few of those thru-hike the entire route in one go, but many hike the trail in sections – a few months, or weeks, at a time.

The Drive » Thirty miles north of Springer Mountain by foot is your first stop in civilization, but if you're on wheels, it's 65 miles by car down graded roads. Take Service Rd 42, make a right on GA 60 and a left on GA 19. Always check road conditions before starting out. Sometimes roads are closed or impassable due to weather.

❸ Mountain Crossings at Walasi-Yi

The one and only constructed intrusion on the trail is the **Mountain Crossings at Walasi-Yi** (www.mountaincrossings.com; 12471 Gainesville Hwy). Of course, parched and sore hikers will be happy it isn't a mirage, as they follow the AT directly through the store, which has served as an outfitter to AT hikers since it was completed by the New Deal's Civilian Conservation Corps in 1937. There are hostel beds for those who'd like to do the first part of the trail and then hike (or hitchhike) back to Springer Mountain. And if you're a thru-hiker and have already blown through gear or forgotten something vital, they'll have it here.

The Drive » Take US 19 for about 22 miles from Mountain Crossings to Dahlonega.

❹ Dahlonega

In the 1820s the Dahlonega area was the site of the country's first gold rush. Its story is told inside the oldest courthouse in Georgia, built in 1836, and home of the **Dahlonega Courthouse Gold Museum** (www.gastateparks.org/dahlonegagoldmuseum; Public Sq). But the new boom can be seen in the thousands of acres of vineyards that lace the surrounding mountainsides. **Naturally Georgia** (www.naturallygeorgia.com; 90 Public Sq N), on the courthouse square, is a combined tasting room and art gallery where they pour surprisingly good dry whites and Portuguese reds from Tiger Mountain (you can find them in Whole Foods in north Georgia) and Crane Creek (a vintner who only sells locally). Or you could simply head to one of dozens of nearby vineyards for a tasting. **Frogtown Cellars** (www.frogtownwine.com; 700 Ridge Point Dr) is a beautiful winery and has a killer deck on which to sip libations and nibble cheese. **Three Sisters** (www.threesistersvineyards.com; 439 Vineyard Way)

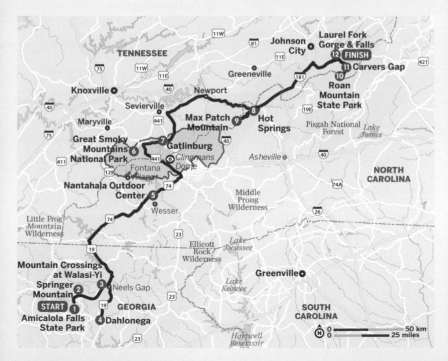

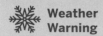

is as unpretentious as it is quirky, where fine wine is paired with bluegrass, overalls and Cheetos.

The Drive » It's a gorgeous 90-mile drive up GA 19 through Vogel State Park and the Blue Ridge Mountains into North Carolina. Hang a right on US 74 to Bryson City.

❺ Nantahala Outdoor Center

Go wild at your next stop, the **Nantahala Outdoor Center** (NOC; www.noc.com; 13077 Hwy 19 W), where the AT and the Nantahala River meet. Nestled in a steep gorge, the river offers 8 miles of easy class II rapids before splashing through exciting class III white water at **Nantahala Falls**. The NOC is a campus, with an outdoor store, an adventure center and a lodge. It also has free trail maps and tips. The AT cuts through the parking lot beside the outdoor store, then crosses the river on the pedestrian bridge. From the NOC it's a 4-mile (strenuous!) hike one way to **Jump Up**, a rocky outcrop boasting outstanding views, or a 6.5-mile hike to the top of **Wesser Bald** (4627ft) and the former fire tower, now an observation deck, offering panoramic views of the Great Smoky Mountains. Hiking north, it's a longer, more strenuous hike (8.1 miles) to the summit of **Cheoah Bald** (5062ft), which offers splendid panoramas of the Southern Appalachians. There are AT sleeping shelters all along the trails for overnight hikers.

The Drive » It's a lovely 25 miles up US 74E to US 441N into Tennessee and the Great Smoky Mountains National Park.

❻ Great Smoky Mountains National Park

This 815-sq-mile park (p60) is America's most visited, but studies have shown that 95% of visitors never venture further than

100yd from their cars, so it's easy to leave the teeming masses behind. In total there are 842 miles of trails in the Great Smoky Mountains National Park, including 73 miles of the AT, which acts as a border between North Carolina and Tennessee. **Clingmans Dome** (6643ft) is almost dead center in the park, and is its highest point. The easiest way to get here is to take US 441 to Clingmans Dome Rd – a 7-mile spur road that ends in a paved parking lot. From there it's a mere half-mile walk to the peak. **Sugarlands Visitor Center** (www.nps.gov/grsm; 107 Park Headquarters Rd) is a great resource for travelers. You can get backcountry permits ($4 per night) and reserve your campsite here. It has loads of maps and advice, and behind the visitor center is a mile-long nature trail to the modest but lovely **Cataract Falls**.

The Drive » It's a quick 3 miles down US 441 from Sugarlands Visitor Center to the heart of downtown Gatlinburg.

❼ Gatlinburg

Wildly kitschy Gatlinburg hunkers at the entrance to the Great Smoky Mountains National Park, waiting to stun hikers with the scent of fudge and cotton candy. Tourists flock here to ride the gondola, get married at the many wedding chapels and sample flavored moonshine. Love it or hate it, the entire village is a gin-u-wine American roadside attraction. A ski or snow-tube area in the winter and an alpine slide in the summer time, Ober Gatlinburg offers one of the best activities in town with its **aerial tramway** (www.obergatlinburg.com; 1001 Parkway). Families love the ride to the lodge at the top of the mountain in the glassed-in gondola, and enjoy coming down even more. **Ole Smoky Moonshine** (www.olesmoky.com; 903 Parkway) is a stone-and-wood moonshine distillery where you can peer over oak barrels and copper boilers and then taste the fiery hooch, which comes in a wild array of flavors, including apple pie and mountain java.

The Drive » Take TN 73 east to TN 32 into Newport, where you'll turn onto US 70 east into Cherokee National Forest and back over the North Carolina state line.

❽ Hot Springs

Hot Springs is known for its steaming, frothing mineral water upwelling from the earth to heal you. **Hot Springs Spa & Mineral Baths** (www.nchotsprings.com; 315 Bridge St) has 17 outdoor riverfront hot tubs fed by natural springs that range from 100°F to 104°F, plus massage rooms and a pre- or post-massage fire pit for relaxing. Want to hit the river? **Hot Springs Rafting Company** (www.hotspringsraftingco.com; 81 Bridge St) will set you up. Take a 5-mile guided trip down the French Broad River on class IIs and IIIs, or brave a 9-mile trip with class IVs. To float at your own pace, hop into a funyak (an inflatable, open-cockpit kayak; adult/child $35/30) or inner tube ($15).

The Drive » It's a brilliant 45-minute mountain drive from the springs to a bald peak. Take NC 209 south for about 7 miles from Hot Springs, turning west onto NC 1175 for 5.3 miles, then turn onto Max Patch Rd (NC 1182). The parking area at the foot of the bald is 3 miles down Max Patch Rd.

❾ Max Patch Mountain

While there's pleasant hiking both north and south, the 1.6-mile round-trip hike, accessed from a trailhead on Max Patch Rd, offers the best payoff for the least amount of sweat. The **Short Loop Trail** winds up the AT's southernmost bald, Max Patch Mountain. From atop the grassy summit there are panoramic views of the Blacks, Balds and Balsams, and the Great Smoky Mountains, of course. On a clear day you can even see the highest point in the eastern US – **Mt Mitchell** (6684ft).

RITU MANOJ JETHAN /SHUTTERSTOCK ©

Aerial tramway, Gatlinburg

Clingmans Dome

Although it may be tempting to drive up the Dome, it's much sweeter to sweat your way to the summit – especially since you'll be hiking a 7.7-mile slice of the AT that begins in Newfound Gap. Sure, the trail parallels the road in sections, but don't let that dissuade you, and if you'd rather not walk down the mountain, you can easily hitch a ride back.

Add another mile, pick up the peak, and enjoy even more scenic beauty on the **Long Loop Trail**.

The Drive » Hop over the border to Tennessee, then continue another 50 miles on TN 352 and I-26. Take exit 32 to reach Roan Mountain State Park.

⑩ Roan Mountain State Park

Roan Mountain State Park (http://tn stateparks.com/parks/about/roan-mountain; 1015 NC 143, Roan Mountain) encompasses 2006 acres of southern Appalachian forest at the base of 6285ft Roan Mountain. On the top of the mountain, straddling the Tennessee–North Carolina border, are the ruins of the old **Cloudland Hotel** site. The 300-room hotel was built in 1885 by Civil War general John T Wilder. Legend has it that North Carolinian sheriffs would hang out in the saloon, waiting for drinkers from the Tennessee side to stray across the line, as North Carolina was a dry state back then. There's also a great 4.6-mile round-trip hike to **Little Rock Knob** (4918ft) through hardwood forests, with epic cliff-top views into Tennessee.

The Drive » Just 8 miles past Roan Mountain State Park on NC 143 you'll reach Carvers Gap.

⑪ Carvers Gap

Carvers Gap is where a set of log steps leads to a section of the AT that crosses a 10-mile series of grassy balds – treeless mountains with unobstructed views over Tennessee's Blue Ridge Mountains. Theories for their creation include everything from extensive grazing to intercession by aliens. To the south, the AT climbs to the high point of the Roan Mountain ridge, the 6285ft **Roan High Knob**.

The Drive » It's just a 27-mile drive through Cherokee National Forest between trailheads. Take NC 143 north and turn left onto TN 37 north.

⑫ Laurel Fork Gorge & Falls

Two moderately taxing hikes lead to Laurel Fork Gorge and Falls. The gorge's vertical walls rise 100ft on either side of the AT, the only trail through the gorge. You can access it, and the 40ft falls, via one of two feeder trails. The first is a 5-mile round trip, the other a 2.6-mile round trip. To hike the former, access the blue-blazed **Hampton Blueline Trail** where I-321 crosses Laurel Fork in Hampton, TN (there's a parking lot for hikers here). The shorter hike can be reached by taking TN 67 from Hampton to Braemar, where you can pick up USFS 50 (Dennis Cove Rd) for just over 3 miles to the parking area on the left. Both hikes use the AT and, with the exception of the steep and quite rocky descent to the falls – which can be treacherous – it's quite flat and easy.

Below: Carvers Gap; Bottom: Roan Mountain State Park

ZACK FRANK/SHUTTERSTOCK ©

Hot Springs National Park

Hot Springs borders a shady, attractive town of the same name that has made an industry out of sharing the park's major resource: mineral-rich waters issuing from hot springs. The healing 143°F (62°C) waters have attracted everyone from Native Americans to early-20th-century health nuts, and it has become known as the 'American Spa.'

Great For...

State
Arkansas

Entrance Fee
Free

Area
8.7 sq miles

Spa Experiences

Spa service Hot Springs–style was never distressingly luxurious, and you get the historical treatment at **Buckstaff Bathhouse** (☏501-623-2308; www.buckstaffbaths. com; 509 Central Ave; thermal bath $33, with massage $71; ⊗8-11:45am daily, plus 1:30-3pm Mon-Sat Mar-Nov, 8-11:45am Mon-Sat, plus 1:30-3pm Mon-Fri Dec-Feb). No-nonsense staff whip you through the baths, treatments and massages, just as in the 1930s. Truly, it's wonderful.

Historical Sights

A promenade runs through the park around the hillside behind Hot Springs' **Bathhouse Row**, where some springs survive intact, and a network of trails covers the town's mountains. Many of the old bathhouses have been converted into art galleries affiliated with the National Park Service.

Learn about the sinful glory days of Prohibition at the **Gangster Museum of**

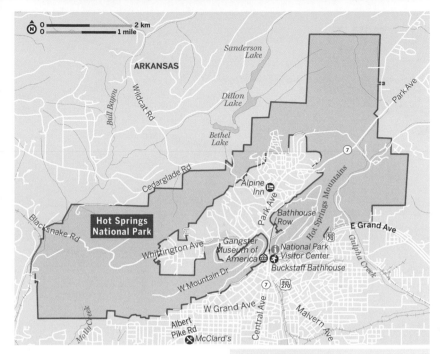

America (501-318-1717; www.tgmoa.com; 510 Central Ave; adult/child $15/6; 10am-5pm Sun-Thu, to 6pm Fri & Sat). This small town in the middle of nowhere turned into a hotbed of lavish wealth thanks to Chicago bootleggers like Capone and his NYC counterparts.

Sleeping & Eating

While the heyday of the Hot Springs spa craze may have passed, there are still some gorgeous old hotels here.

The friendly Scottish owners of the **Alpine Inn** (501-624-9164; www.alpine-inn-hot-springs.com; 741 Park Ave; r $69-99;), located less than a mile from Bathhouse Row, have spent a few years upgrading an old motel to remarkable ends. The rooms are impeccable, comfortable and include flat-screen TVs and sumptuous beds.

Restaurants congregate along the Central Ave tourist strip in Hot Springs. The **Colonial**

Essential Information

On Bathhouse Row in the 1915 Fordyce Bathhouse, the **NPS visitor center** (501-620-6715; www.nps.gov/hosp; 369 Central Ave; 9am-5pm) FREE has exhibits about park history.

Buses head from Hot Springs to Little Rock with **Greyhound** (501-623-5574; www.greyhound.com; 100 Broadway Tce; 1½ hours, from $13, around three daily). The town is off I-30, about 60 miles southwest of Little Rock.

Pancake House (501-624-9273; 111 Central Ave; mains $6-10; 7am-3pm) is a Hot Springs classic, with turquoise booths and homey touches like quilts and doilies on the walls, almost like your grandma's kitchen.

On the outskirts of downtown Hot Springs, Bill Clinton's favorite boyhood barbecue, **McClard's** (501-623-9665; www.mcclards.com; 505 Albert Pike; mains $4-15; 11am-8pm Tue-Sat), is still popular. ∎

Top left: Ozark bathhouse, Hot Springs; Bottom left: Natural hot spring

Top right: Stained glass ceiling, Fordyce Bathhouse (p87); Bottom right: Buckstaff Bathhouse (p86)

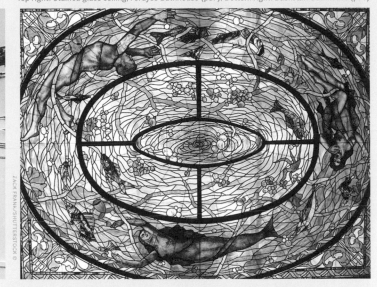

ZACK FRANK/SHUTTERSTOCK ©

CLASSIC ROAD TRIPS

Natchez Trace Parkway

America grew from infancy to adolescence in the late 18th and 19th centuries. That's when it explored and expanded, traded and clashed with Native Americans, and eventually confronted its own shadow during the Civil War. Evidence of this drama borders the Natchez Trace, an ancient footpath transformed into a (now NPS-designated) parkway by the Civilian Conservation Corps in the 1930s. Before you begin, hit Nashville's honky-tonks for rollicking country music.

Distance 444 miles/715km

Duration 3 days

Best Time to Go
The climate is lovely in spring (April to June) and fall (September to November).

Essential Photo
Emerald Mound, one of the country's largest Native American mounds, just before sunset.

Best for History
Touring the Civil War–era Carter House in Franklin.

❶ Nashville
Although this leafy, sprawling Southern city – with its thriving economy and hospitable locals – has no scarcity of charms, it really is all about the music. Boot-stomping honky-tonks lure aspiring stars from across the country, all of them hoping to ascend into the royalty on display at the **Country Music Hall of Fame** (www.countrymusichalloffame.org; 222 5th Ave S). Don't miss **Bluebird Cafe** (www.bluebirdcafe.com; 4104 Hillsboro Pike, Green Hills), tucked into a suburban strip mall. No chitchat in this singer-songwriter haven, or you'll get bounced. Enjoy a less-controlled musical environment at **Tootsie's Orchid Lounge** (www.tootsies.net; 422 Broadway), a glorious dive smothered with old photographs and handbills from the Nashville Sound's glory days. Bluegrass fans will adore **Station Inn** (www.stationinn.com; 402 12th Ave S), where you'll sit at a small cocktail table, swill beer (only), and marvel at the lightning fingers of fine bluegrass players. Before hopping onto the Natchez Trace, fuel up with country ham and red-eye gravy at the **Loveless Cafe** (www.lovelesscafe.com; 8400 TN 100), beside the start of the parkway. It's been serving Southern fare to travelers for more than 65 years.

The Drive ≫ Heading south, you will traverse the Double-Arch Bridge, 155ft above the valley, before settling in for a pleasant country drive on the parkway. You'll notice dense woods encroaching and arching elegantly over the baby-bottom-smooth highway for the next 444 miles. It's about 10 miles from Nashville to Franklin.

❷ Franklin
Before you embark on the Trace, consider a sidetrip to Franklin, just 10 miles outside Nashville. The Victorian-era downtown of this tiny historic hamlet is charming, and the nearby artsy enclave of **Leiper's Fork** is fun and eclectic. But you're in the area to check out one of the Civil War's bloodiest battlefields. On November 30, 1864, 37,000 men (20,000 Confederates and 17,000 Union soldiers) fought over a two-mile stretch of Franklin's outskirts. Nashville's sprawl has turned much of that battlefield into suburbs, but you can see a preserved eight-acre chunk at the **Carter House**

(www.boft.org; 1140 Columbia Ave, Franklin), still riddled with 1000-plus bullet holes.

The Drive » The parkway carves a path through dense woodland as you swerve past another historic district at Leiper's Fork, before coming to the first of several Old Trace turnouts after about 40 miles.

❸ Old Trace

At Mile 403.7 (don't mind the 'backward' mile markers, we think a north–south route works best) you'll find the first of several sections of the Old Trace. In the early 19th century, Kaintucks (boatmen from Ohio and Pennsylvania) floated coal, livestock and agricultural goods down the Ohio and Mississippi Rivers aboard flat-bottom boats. Often their boats were emptied in Natchez, where they disembarked and began the long walk home up the Old Trace to Nashville, where they could access established roads further north. This path intersected Choctaw and Chickasaw country, which meant it was hazardous. In fact,

indigenous travelers were the first to beat this earth. You can walk a 2000ft section of that original trail at this turnout.

The Drive » There follows a beautiful 20-mile stretch of road, as the parkway flows past Baker Bluff (Mile 405.1), a pull-off with views over Duck River. Just south, a parking lot for Jackson Falls (Mile 404.7) can be reached by a short, steep trail (900ft one way). You can also hike to the falls from Baker Bluff, it just takes a little longer.

❹ Meriwether Lewis Site

At Mile 385.9, you'll come to the Meriwether Lewis Site, where the famed explorer and first governor of the Louisiana territory died mysteriously at **Grinders Inn**. His fateful journey began in September, 1809, and his plan was to travel to Washington, DC to defend his spending of government funds (think of it as an early-days subpoena before a Congressional committee). At Fort Pickering, a remote wilderness outpost near modern-day Memphis, he met up with

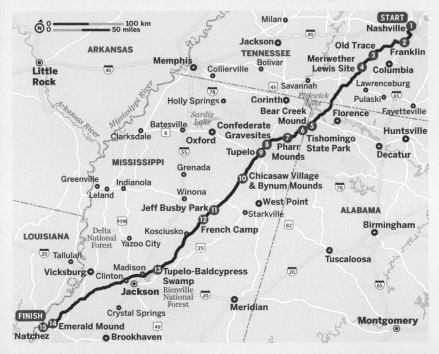

a Chickasaw agent named James Neely, who was to escort the Lewis party safely through Chickasaw land. They traveled north, through the bush, and along the Old Trace to **Grinder's Stand**, and checked into the inn run by the pioneering Grinder family. Mrs Grinder made up a room for Lewis and fed him, and after he retired, two shots rang out. The legendary explorer was shot in the head and chest and died at 35. Lewis' good friend, Thomas Jefferson, was convinced it was suicide. His family disagreed. His grave marker is in the pioneer cemetery at the back of the adjacent loop road. The inn no longer stands, but a small cabin at the site, staffed by guides, has a few exhibits (9am to 4:30pm Friday to Sunday mid-March to mid-September).

The Drive » It's about 77 miles to your next stop. You'll cross into Alabama at Mile 341.8. In Alabama, music buffs can detour to Muscle Shoals, where producers and local studios worked with Bob Dylan, the Rolling Stones, Otis Redding, Aretha Franklin, Wilson Pickett and other artists. You'll cross into Mississippi at Mile 308.

❺ Bear Creek Mound

Just across the Alabama state line in Mississippi, at Mile 308.8, you'll find Bear Creek Mound, an ancient indigenous ceremonial site. There are seven groups of Native American mounds found along the parkway, all of them in Mississippi. Varying in shape from Maya-like pyramids to domes to small rises, they were used for worship and burying the dead; a number were seen as power spots for local chiefs who sometimes lived on top of them. That was arguably the case at Bear Creek, which was built between 1100 and 1300 CE. Archaeologists are convinced that there was a temple and/or a chief's dwelling at the top of the rise.

The Drive » The highway bisects Tishomingo State Park at Mile 304.5.

❻ Tishomingo State Park

Named for the Chickasaw Chief Tishomingo, this lovely **park** (https://mississippi stateparks.reserveamerica.com; Mile 304.

5 Natchez Trace Pkwy, Tishomingo) is an inviting place to camp and explore. It's home to evocative, moss-covered sandstone cliffs and rock formations, fern gullies, waterfalls in Bear Creek canyon and a photogenic suspension bridge built by the Civilian Conservation Corps in the 1930s. Hiking trails abound, and you can paddle **Bear Creek** in a rented canoe. Wildflowers bloom in spring. It's a special oasis, and one that was utilized by the Chickasaw and their Paleo-Indian antecedents. Evidence of their civilization in the park dates back to 7000 BCE.

The Drive » Just under 20 miles of more wooded beauty leads from Tishomingo State Park to the next stop, a series of Native American mounds at Mile 286.7.

❼ Pharr Mounds

This is a 2000-year-old, 90-acre complex of eight indigenous burial sites. Four were excavated in 1966 and found to have fireplaces and low platforms where the dead were cremated. Ceremonial artifacts were also found, along with copper vessels, which raised some eyebrows. Copper is not indigenous to Mississippi, and its presence here indicates an extensive trade network with other nations and peoples.

The Drive » About 17 miles on, at Mile 269.4, you'll come across a turnout that links up to another section of the Old Trace and offers a bit more recent history.

❽ Confederate Gravesites

Just north of Tupelo, on a small rise overlooking the Old Trace, lies a row of 13 graves of unknown Confederate soldiers. What led to their fate has been lost in time. Some believe they died during the Confederate retreat from Corinth, Mississippi, following the legendary Battle of Shiloh; others think they were wounded in the nearby Battle of Brice's Crossroads, and buried by their brothers here.

The Drive » Less than 10 miles later you will loop into the comparatively large hamlet of Tupelo, at Mile 266, where you can gather road supplies for the south-ward push.

⑨ Tupelo

Here, the **Natchez Trace Parkway Visitor Center** (www.nps.gov/natr; Mile 266 Natchez Trace Pkwy) is a fantastic resource with good natural- and American-history displays, and detailed parkway maps. Tupelo is world famous for its favorite son, and **Elvis Presley's Birthplace** (www.elvispresleybirthplace. com; 306 Elvis Presley Dr) is a pilgrimage site for those who kneel before the King. The original structure has a new roof and furniture, but no matter the decor – it was within these humble walls that Elvis was born on January 8, 1935, learned to play the guitar and began to dream big. His family's church, where he was first bitten by the music bug, has been transported and restored here too. Inside the welcoming

Tupelo Hardware Co (www.facebook.com/ tupelohardware; 114 W Main St), you can stand where Elvis stood when he bought his first guitar – an X marks the spot.

The Drive » Barely out of Tupelo, at Mile 261.8, is Chickasaw Village. The Bynum Mounds are nearly another 30 miles south. You'll see the turn off just after leaving the Tombigbee National Forest.

⑩ Chicasaw Village & Bynum Mounds

South from Tupelo, the Trace winds past the **Chickasaw Village** site, where displays document how the Chickasaw lived and traveled during the fur-trade heyday of the early 19th century. It was 1541 when Hernando de Soto entered Mississippi under the Spanish flag. They fought a bitter battle, and though De Soto survived, the Chickasaw held strong. By the 1600s the

Elvis Presley's Birthplace

English had engaged the Chickasaw in what became a lucrative fur trade. Meanwhile, the French held sway just west in the massive Louisiana Territory. As allies to England, the Chickasaw found themselves up against not only the French, but their Choctaw allies.

Further down the road is the site of six 2100-year-old **Bynum Mounds**. Five were excavated just after WWII, and copper tools and cremated remains were found. Two of the mounds have been restored for public viewing.

The Drive » It's about 39 miles from the Bynum Mounds to Jeff Busby Park at Mile 193.1.

⑪ Jeff Busby Park

Don't miss this hilltop park with picnic tables and a fabulous overlook taking in low-lying, forested hills that extend for miles. Exhibits at the top include facts and figures about local flora and fauna, as well as a primer on indigenous tools. **Little Mountain Trail**, a half-mile loop that takes 30 minutes to complete, descends from the parking lot into a shady hollow. Another half-mile spur trail branches from that loop to the campground below.

The Drive » Thirteen miles down the road, near Mile 180, the forest clears and an agrarian plateau emerges, jade-hued and perfect, as if this land has been cultivated for centuries.

⑫ French Camp

In the hamlet of French Camp, the site of a former French pioneer settlement, you can walk around an antebellum home, built by Revolutionary War veteran Colonel James Drane. Nearby it's possible to check out the ornate stagecoach of Greenwood LeFlore, which carried the last chief of the Choctaw nation east of the Mississippi on his two trips to Washington to negotiate with President Andrew Jackson. For locally made crafts, step into the **Log Cabin Gift Shop**. Sandwiches, soup and desserts are served at the attached Council Cafe (10:30am to

8pm Monday to Saturday; sandwiches $8 to $10). The gift shop and cafe are run by French Camp Academy, a Christian boarding school nearby.

The Drive » As you head south, the forest clears for snapshot scenes of horses on the prairie, before the trees encroach again and again. The next stop is about 55 miles down the Trace. You'll pass Kosciusko, the birthplace and childhood hometown of media star Oprah Winfrey, at Mile 150.

⑬ Tupelo-Baldcypress Swamp

At Mile 122, you can examine some of these trees up close as you tour the stunning Tupelo-Baldcypress Swamp. The 20-minute **trail** snakes through an abandoned channel and continues on a boardwalk over the milky green swamp shaded by water tupelo and bald cypresses. Look for turtles on the rocks and gators in the murk.

The Drive » The swamp empties into the Ross R Barnett Reservoir, visible to the east as you roll toward the state capital of Jackson. Exit the parkway at Old Canton Rd for arts and crafts at the **Mississippi Craft Center** (950 Rice Rd). Beyond Jackson, there is a photogenic section of sunken trace at Mile 41.5.

⑭ Emerald Mound

Near Mile 10.3, accessible by a graded road leading west from the parkway, the eye-catching **Emerald Mound** (www.nps. gov/natr; Mile 10.3 Natchez Trace Pkwy) is by far the best of the indigenous mound sites. Using stone tools, pre-Columbian ancestors to the Natchez people graded this eight-acre mountain into a flat-topped pyramid. It is now one of the largest mounds in North America. There are shady, creekside picnic spots, and if you climb to the top you'll find a vast lawn along with a diagram of what the temple may have looked like. It would have been perched on the secondary and highest of the mounds. A visit here is a perfect diversion on an easy spring afternoon just before the sun smolders, when birdsong rings from the trees and mingles with the call of a distant train.

The Drive » Drive on for about 13 more miles. As you approach Natchez, the mossy arms of southern oaks spread over the roadway, and the air gets just a touch warmer and more moist. You can almost smell the river from here.

⑮ Natchez

When the woods part, revealing historic antebellum mansions, you have reached Natchez. In the 1840s, Natchez had more millionaires per capita than any city in the world (because the plantation owners didn't pay their staff). Opulent and undeniably beautiful, these homes were built on the backs of slave labor. The mansions open for tours in the spring and fall 'pilgrimage seasons,' and some are open year-round. Tours of the Greek Revival **Melrose** (www.nps.gov/natc; 1 Melrose-Montebello Pkwy) house take a multi-perspective look at life on the city estate of a slave-owning cotton magnate.

Natchez has dirt under its fingernails, too. When Mark Twain came through (which he did on numerous occasions), he crashed in a room above the local watering hole. **Under the Hill Saloon** (25 Silver St), across the street from the mighty Mississippi River, remains the best bar in town, with terrific live music on weekends. Above the hill, you'll find beer and live music at **Smoot's** (www.smootsgrocery.com; 319 N Broadway St), a former grocery now re-imagined as a juke joint.

STEVENGERTNER/GETTY IMAGES ©

Historic mansion, Natchez

ZACK FRANK/SHUTTERSTOCK ©

Mammoth Cave National Park

Home to the longest cave system on earth, Mammoth Cave National Park has more than 400 miles of surveyed passageways. Mammoth is at least three times longer than any other known cave, with vast interior cathedrals, bottomless pits and undulating rock formations. Guided tours delve into its spookily beautiful underworld.

Great For...

State
Kentucky

Entrance Fee
Free; cave tours $6–60

Area
83 sq miles

Cave Tours

The caves have been used for prehistoric mineral gathering, as a source of saltpeter for gunpowder and as a tuberculosis hospital.

The only way to see them is on a ranger-guided tour. Options range from hour-long subterranean strolls to strenuous, day-long spelunking adventures. The **Frozen Niagara Tour** is the easiest, offering glimpses of groovy formations in large caverns. The popular **Domes and Dripstones Tour** takes in several dramatic deposits, though you must go up and down 500 stairs and squeeze through tight areas. The magical **Violet City Tour** takes place by lantern light. There's a specialty accessible tour option too.

Book tours online at www.recreation. gov; advance tickets are wise in summer. It's always chilly in the caves, so bring a sweater.

Hiking

Eighty-five miles of trails stripe the park's forested hills. The 3.5-mile **Turnhole Bend Trail** winds through old-growth stands of oaks and hickories and past secluded bluffs. The 2-mile **Cedar Sink Trail** offers the requisite cliffs and trees, plus wildflowers and odd-looking sinkholes. Most trails make for fairly easy trekking.

Canoeing & Kayaking

The Green River moseys through the park for 25 miles, as does the Nolin River for 6 miles. They're prime for paddling, carrying visitors on a slow-moving current past dramatic cliffs, towering trees and wildlife such as beavers, foxes and wild turkeys. Several outfitters rent canoes and kayaks and can set up excursions ranging from three hours to three days (with camping on river islands). The park's website has contact details.

Essential Information

The **visitor center** (270-758-2180; www.nps.gov/maca; 1 Mammoth Cave Pkwy; 8.30am-4.30pm) has trail maps and cave tour tickets.

The park lies a short distance west of I-65, halfway between Louisville, KY and Nashville, TN.

Camping

For overnight stays, there are three basic campgrounds with restrooms (sites from $20; reserve at www.recreation. gov); 13 free backcountry campsites (get a permit at the park visitor center); and a hotel and cottages (reserve at www. mammothcavelodge.com). ■

CLASSIC ROAD TRIPS

Civil Rights Tour

To trace the solemn, sad, yet triumphant road of American civil rights activists is to explore the very worst and the incomparable best of America. Following Dr Martin Luther King Jr's journey from his Atlanta birthplace and biblical upbringing to his assassination in Memphis visits the stages of Montgomery, Selma and Birmingham and reveals, within the human experience, an infinite capacity to love, endure and cultivate strength and faith no matter what.

This trip takes in, among other sites, a range of NPS-designated historic sites and monuments.

Distance 568 miles/914km

Duration 4 days

Best Time to Go
Avoid April to June to dodge the crowds.

Essential Photo
The Edmund Pettus Bridge at sunset has an eerie, solemn beauty.

Best for History
The National Memorial for Peace & Justice, when combined with the Legacy Museum, provides a powerful context for understanding America.

❶ Atlanta
The story begins in Atlanta, where the **Sweet Auburn** neighborhood was already a bustling, affluent, middle-class beacon of African American advancement in the oppressive, segregated South when a preacher's son, Martin Luther King Jr, was born here on January 15, 1929. You can visit the **Martin Luther King Jr Birthplace** (501 Auburn Ave) on a guided tour, one of several sights that form the **Martin Luther King Jr National Historic Site** (www.nps.gov/malu; 450 Auburn Ave), Atlanta's civil rights nexus. First, get a powerful civil rights primer at the **visitor center**, where dehumanizing segregation-era laws are etched into glass. Across the street is the **First Ebenezer Baptist Church** (407 Auburn Ave NE), where King's father led the congregation, and his mother directed the choir. Sit on a wooden pew and listen to Dr King's voice echo through the serene sanctuary of a 1963 time capsule. Nearby, King is entombed in the courtyard behind the nonprofit **King Center for Nonviolent Social Change** (www.thekingcenter.org; 449 Auburn Ave NE), where there's a small gallery on the 2nd floor worth seeing.

The Drive » It's a two-hour drive south on I-85 across the state line and into Alabama to reach Tuskegee.

❷ Tuskegee
Before the Civil Rights movement of the 1950s and 1960s, there were the Tuskegee Airmen. Also known as the Red Tails, these African American fighter pilots – America's first – shattered the glass ceiling and received their training at what is now the **Tuskegee Airmen National Historic Site** (www.nps.gov/tuai; 1616 Chappie James Rd) in July 1941. The first graduating class had 13 cadets, but eventually over 300 African American pilots were trained here and served overseas. Their legacy is important because African American soldiers who had served in Europe enjoyed freedoms there that they were denied at home, and many began to work diligently for desegregation upon returning to the South after the war. Tuskegee is also the home of Booker T Washington's **Tuskegee Institute**, which was America's first African American

teacher's college, as well as a noted agricultural institute. George Washington Carver – the famed agricultural pioneer who developed alternative crops to cotton such as peanuts and soy – taught and published here for 47 years; there is a **museum** (www.nps.gov/tuin; University Campus Ave) dedicated to him.

The Drive » Continue southwest on I-85 for another 45 minutes to reach Montgomery, Alabama's capital city.

❸ Montgomery

Montgomery, AL, was the heart of the mid-20th-century Civil Rights movement, and the heart of Montgomery now hosts one of the most comprehensive accounts of the Black struggle for equal rights in America. Brooding on a hill in the center of town, the **National Memorial for Peace & Justice** (National Lynching Memorial; www.eji.org/national-lynching-memorial; 417 Caroline St) is a testament wrought in stone and steel to thousands of Black victims of lynchings across American history. Rusty steel slabs, inscribed with the names of the dead, are a mute, powerful witness to decades of communal violence.

Nearby (you can take a shuttle, or a pleasant 15-minute walk), the **Legacy Museum** (http://museumandmemorial.eji.org; 115 Coosa St) contextualizes the Black American experience from slavery to the modern day, and demonstrates how past disenfranchisement (ie voter registration suppression) remains relevant today. If you want to go further back in time, Rosa Parks' act of iconic resistance is recreated at the **Rosa Parks Museum** (www.troy.edu/rosaparks; 251 Montgomery St), located in the former site of the Empire Theater, in front of which Parks took her defiant stand.

Finally, for those tracing the life of Dr Martin Luther King Jr, Montgomery is the spot to visit the **Dexter Avenue Parsonage** (www.dexterkingmemorial.org/tours/parsonage-museum; 309 S Jackson St) and **King Memorial Church** (www.dexterkingmemorial.org;

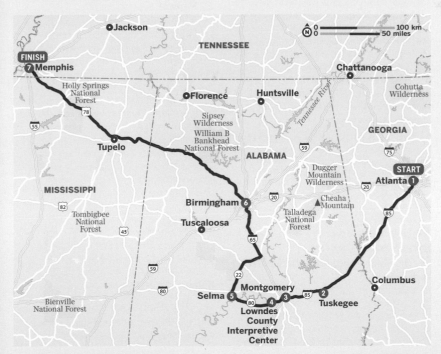

Rosa Parks' Targeted Activism

Rosa Parks' decision to stand – or sit, as the case was – firm when asked to vacate her seat in the whites-only section of a Montgomery bus has long been portrayed as an act of spontaneous defiance. But Parks was no church lady who just wanted to rest her feet. She was an experienced activist and had a history of engaging in targeted civil disobedience. She was also a member of the National Association for the Advancement of Colored People (NAACP) and had trained with colleagues at a retreat held not long before her admirable defiance. Parks never lost her penchant for activism and community organizing, even well into her later retirement.

454 Dexter Ave); both places were important nodes of stability during King's fight for equal rights and representation.

Close to the Alabama Capitol steps is the **Civil Rights Memorial Center** (www.spl center.org/civil-rights-memorial; 400 Washington Ave). The memorial is a circular fountain designed by Maya Lin – who also designed the Vietnam Veterans Memorial – and a haunting remembrance of 40 martyrs of the movement, all activists or citizens murdered for their convictions, deeds or simply their color.

The Drive » US 80 is a straight shot west into Alabama's old cotton country. You are now traveling one of the Civil Rights movement's darkest and most divisive roads, and it leads to Selma. After 30 miles, you'll reach the Lowndes County Interpretive Center.

❹ Lowndes County Interpretive Center

The **Selma to Montgomery National Historic Trail** (US 80; www.nps.gov/semo) commemorates the 1965 Voting Rights March, one of the most violent and contentious of Alabama's civil rights confrontations. During voting-rights activities in nearby Dallas County, a young activist, Jimmie Lee

Jackson, was shot and killed at point-blank range while attempting to shelter his mother from police batons during a peaceful march. In his memory, the Dallas County Voting Rights League decided to walk from Selma to Montgomery to highlight police brutality, and invited King and the Southern Christian Leadership Conference (SCLC) to join them. But another violent police crackdown in Selma halted the march. A second attempt was made, but King turned the marchers back fearing for their safety. Finally, the march succeeded on its third attempt. Halfway between Montgomery and Selma, the **Lowndes County Interpretive Center** (www.nps.gov/semo; 7002 US Hwy 80) is a wonderfully done museum, where a 25-minute documentary delves into the march. This site was also integral to the movement's next phase. The seeds of Black Power were sown here after the march was over.

The Drive » Stay on US 80 east for about 21 miles until you reach Selma.

❺ Selma

On March 7, 1965, aka 'Bloody Sunday,' Alabama State troopers and recently deputized local white men attacked 500 peaceful marchers on the **Edmund Pettus Bridge** (Broad St & Water Ave) with clubs and tear gas. The whole thing was captured on video, marking one of the first times Americans outside the South had witnessed the horrifying images of the struggle. Shock and outrage was widespread, and support for the movement grew. Eventually President Lyndon Johnson ordered the Alabama National Guard to protect what became over 8000 marchers (singer-songwriter Joan Baez famously walked among them) who poured in from across the country to walk the 54 miles in four days, beginning on March 16 and culminating with a classic King speech on the capitol steps.

Near the base of the Pettus Bridge, the **Selma Interpretive Center** (www.nps. gov/semo; 2 Broad St) provides context and historical background. Just across the river is the more grassroots **National Voting Rights Museum** (www.nvrmi.com; 6 US 80 E).

The bulk of the movement's organization in the 1960s took place at the striking brick-red Victorian church, **Brown Chapel** (www.facebook.com/brownchapelame; 410 Martin Luther King St).

The Drive » From Selma, head east on AL 22, skirt the pine-dappled lake at Paul M Grist State Park, then veer north on AL 191 before merging with US 31 and I-65 north into Birmingham, a total distance of about 90 miles.

❻ Birmingham

Progressive Birmingham was not always so inviting. When Bull Conner was the sheriff, civil rights activists, led by Dr King, embarked on a desegregation campaign downtown that employed masses of 'foot soldiers' – local activists, often high school students, who flooded local jails. Eventually, the Birmingham police responded to civil disobedience with water cannons and attack dogs, creating images that horrified the world, and which are subsequently immortalized via conceptual sculpture in **Kelly Ingram Park** (1600 5th Ave N). The campaign also gave us King's famed 'Letter from Birmingham Jail.'

All of this history is on display at the superb **Birmingham Civil Rights Institute** (www.bcri.org; 520 16th St N). The seven-block **Birmingham Civil Rights Memorial Trail** (www.bcri.org; 520 16th St N), installed in 2013 for the 50th anniversary of the campaign, depicts 22 moving scenes with statues and photography. It begins at the BCRI. The saddest and most enduring memories from that struggle remain the murder of four little girls, killed when the **16th Street Baptist Church** (www.16thstreetbaptist.org; cnr 16th St & 6th Ave N) was bombed by the Ku Klux Klan during Sunday School.

Birmingham Civil Rights Institute

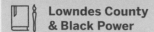

Lowndes County & Black Power

The march from Selma to Montgomery was a watershed moment in the Civil Rights movement, and not simply because of the violence that turned stomachs around the world. It also sparked a rupture between the Student Nonviolent Coordinating Committee (SNCC) and Martin Luther King Jr's Southern Christian Leadership Conference (SCLC).

The SNCC was first on the ground in Selma, and was supporting the Dallas County Voting Rights League when Jimmie Lee Jackson was shot and killed. It invited the SCLC to join them because King's stature allowed them to raise money and receive maximum media attention. Yet some younger SNCC activists, including Stokely Carmichael (who would go on to be a founding member of the Black Panther Party), bristled at what they saw as a takeover of their organizing work, and were especially peeved when King turned the marchers around during their second attempt to cross the Edmund Pettus Bridge. When they eventually passed through Lowndes County on their way to Montgomery, Carmichael promised local folks that SNCC would be back. He kept his promise, and their ensuing voter registration drive saw the number of Lowndes County Blacks registered to vote increase from 70 to 2600 – 300 more than white registered voters. The new party, the Lowndes County Freedom Organization, was the first to employ a black panther as its logo.

The success of Carmichael's registration drive had a ripple effect. Locally, about 40 share-cropping families were evicted from their land by their white landlords after the ensuing election. They set up a tented camp and lived on what is now home to the Lowndes County Interpretive Center. On a national level, within a year, the existing SNCC leadership – closely allied with Dr King – was ousted in favor of Carmichael, who made more waves when he delivered his first 'Black Power' speech in Greenwood, MS, in 1966.

The Drive » From Birmingham take US 78 west for 219 miles through the Holly Springs National Forest and merge onto I-240, which snakes into Memphis.

➐ Memphis

It was here that King's crusade was abruptly halted in April 1968, when he visited Memphis in support of the Black sanitation-workers strike. The visit was tense, and King's entourage noticed he was more nervous than usual. On April 3 he spoke prophetically at the Mason Temple: 'Like anybody, I would like to live a long life... But I'm not concerned about that now... I've seen the Promised Land. I may not get there with you. But I want you to know tonight, that we, as a people, will get to the Promised Land!'

The next day, while standing on the balcony outside room 306 at the **Lorraine Motel** on the south end of downtown Memphis, James Earl Ray shot King in the neck and face. He collapsed, one foot hanging off the railing, and died. Both the Lorraine Motel and the boarding house from where the shot was allegedly fired are now part of the **National Civil Rights Museum** (www. civilrightsmuseum.org; 450 Mulberry St).

Below: National Civil Rights Museum; Bottom: Edmund Pettus Bridge (p100)

African American Civil Rights Network

The National Park Service coordinates a range of properties, facilities and interpretive programs associated with the African American Civil Rights movement in the USA under the African American Civil Rights Network.

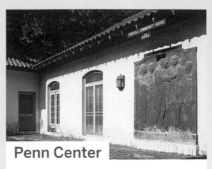

Penn Center

Once the home of one of the first schools for freed slaves, **Penn Center** (www.penncenter.com; 16 Penn Center Circle W, St Helena Island) has a small museum that covers Gullah culture (African American culture from the coasts of Georgie and South Carolina) and the history of Penn School. Two sites on the property are part of the National Reconstruction Era Site: the school building, and Brick Baptist Church, originally constructed by slaves who were not allowed to worship inside. Freed slaves took control of it in 1861.

Little Rock Central High School

The most riveting **historic attraction** (www.nps.gov/chsc; 2125 Daisy L Gatson Bates Dr) in Little Rock, Arkansas, is the site of the 1957 desegregation crisis that changed the country forever. This was where a group of African American students known as the Little Rock Nine were first denied entry to the then all-white high school despite a unanimous 1954 Supreme Court ruling forcing the integration of public schools. Images of the students being escorted to class by national guard soldiers remain some of the most iconic records of the Civil Rights movement.

Medgar & Myrlie Evers Home National Monument

It's hard not to get chills while touring the ranch-style **home** (www.nps.gov/memy; 2332 Margaret Walker Alexandra Dr) where Civil Rights activist Medgar Evers was murdered in 1963. Evers was standing outside the house in Jackson, Mississippi, in the carport when Byron De La Beckwith shot him from across the street. The bullet tore into the house and the bullet holes are still visible. You can read the historic marker on the lawn and some information in the carport, or call house curator Minnie Walson to schedule a tour.

Lorraine Motel

The Lorraine Motel (Memphis, Tennessee), where Martin Luther King Jr was fatally shot on April 4, 1968, now houses part of the gut-wrenching National Civil Rights Museum (p102). Its immersive and compelling exhibits chronicle the struggle for African American freedom and equality from the earliest days of slavery in America. Both Dr King's cultural contribution and his assassination serve as prisms for looking at the Civil Rights movement, its precursors and its continuing impact on American life.

In Focus

The Parks Today 108
A century old and counting, the National Park Service still faces an ongoing battle with outside threats.

History 110
The foresight of a few individuals has created a legacy for millions to enjoy.

Outdoor Activities 116
There's more to the national parks than hiking. Wildly diverse landscapes offer activities to suit every taste.

Flora & Fauna 121
National parks have helped some of America's most iconic animals – bears, wolves, mountain lions, Florida panthers – back from the brink of extinction.

Conservation 127
Safeguarding the parks' treasures has always been a struggle, and today conservationists are facing new challenges.

Landscapes & Geology 130
America's parks are a testament to its violent and spectacular geological history.

Below left: Linville Falls (p76); Below right: Snail kite

The Parks Today

A 2016 anniversary celebrated a century in which the US National Park Service grew from 12 parks to almost 60 (there are now 63). But the following year brought new challenges to the USA's protected areas. And while some of the excesses of the Trump era have been overturned by President Biden, the future for America's parks still looks a little more uncertain than it once did.

Parks under Threat

The Trump administration committed to reducing several protected areas significantly. In Utah, Bears Ears National Monument, which protected land sacred to the Pueblo Indians, the Navajo and the Ute, shrank by around 85%, and 1996-designated Grand Staircase-Escalante National Monument was almost halved in size. The move was unprecedented. While presidents had shrunk national monuments in the past, most recently in the early 1960s, this had never been undertaken on such a significant scale. President Biden reversed the decision when he came into office in 2021. But the whole episode left many reflecting on the precarious nature of America's great natural landscapes all over the country.

Funding the National Parks Service

Despite record-breaking park visitor numbers in 2016, the 2018 federal budget contained cuts of around $300 million to the operating budget of the National Parks Service (NPS), prompting the NPS to warn of possible staff cuts, campground closures, reduced operating hours and reduced services in up to 90% of its parks. After winning the 2020 election, President Biden restored much of the NPS's funding. In 2022 his administration announced a 2023 budget of $3.6 billion for the NPS, an increase of $492.2 million compared to the previous year; the 2020 budget had been $2.7 billion.

Climate Change

Climate change is another existential threat to the national parks in both the near and long-term future, in the form of more intense and frequent wildfires, or in devastating hurricanes in the southeast.

To complicate matters further, in 2022 the conservative majority on the US Supreme Court ruled against the Environmental Protection Agency (EPA) and severely restricted its ability to limit carbon and other emissions from the fossil-fuel industry. Seen as a major blow to any attempts by the federal government to tackle climate change, the court's ruling could have devastating impacts on the health of the nation's ecosystems and its national parks.

Saving the Everglades

The Everglades is one of the most important wilderness areas in the lower 48; a fragile ecosystem rich in astonishing wildlife that is under threat from human-led and natural causes.

This delicate environment neighbors one of the fastest-growing urban areas in the US. The current water-drainage system in South Florida was built to handle the needs of two million people; the local population is now closer to 10 million. Scientists estimate the wetlands have been reduced to as little as a quarter of their original size.

And then there's the growing cast of invasive species. The largest of these is the Burmese python: one specimen found in 2022 was nearly 18ft long and weighed 215lb. Burmese pythons first began turning up in the Everglades in the 1980s; the latest estimates suggest that as many as 300,000 may now live in the wild in southern Florida. They prey on a whole range of species, which could cause many of them to disappear from the region. The number of nesting wading birds has already declined by 90% to 95% since the 1930s. Currently there are more than 60 threatened and endangered plant and animal species in the park.

It's not just about the Everglades. Whether or not this area can be protected from its many threats may well be a bellwether for the future of America's environment.

Yosemite National Park, California

History

Few things are as quintessentially American as national parks. Their genesis, implementation and growth since 1872 is a work of genius second only to the US Constitution. A handful of people once had the foresight to pull the reins in on rampant hunting, logging, mining and tourist development, so that at least some of America's most magnificent treasures might be saved for future generations – their actions constitute one of the greatest chapters in US history.

1864
President Abraham Lincoln designates Yosemite Valley and the Mariposa Grove a protected state park.

1872
President Ulysses S Grant designates Yellowstone the world's first national park.

1890
Yosemite National Park is established, but the state of California retains control of Yosemite Valley and Mariposa Grove.

A Magnificent Park

American portrait artist George Catlin (1796–1872) is credited with being the first person to conceptualize a 'nation's park.' He envisioned a 'magnificent park' to protect the country's remaining indigenous people, buffalo and wilderness from the onslaught of western expansion. But over three decades would pass before anything remotely resembling that vision existed.

In 1851 members of an armed militia accidentally rode into a massive granite valley in the Sierra Nevada (a mountain range in California) and decided to call it 'Yosemity,' possibly a corruption of the Miwok word *Oo-hoo'-ma-te* or *uzumatel*, meaning 'grizzly bear.' The name stuck, and soon word of the valley and its waterfalls got out. Within no time, entrepreneurs were divvying up the land in hopes of profiting from tourists.

Thanks to a handful of outspoken writers, artists, naturalists and – most importantly – the efforts of the great landscape architect Frederick Law Olmsted, Yosemite Valley was spared privatization. In 1864 President Abraham Lincoln signed a bill into law that put

1894	1906	1916
After a poacher is caught killing bison in Yellowstone, Congress grants the park the power to enforce conservation laws.	Mesa Verde becomes the seventh national park and the first dedicated to protecting cultural heritage.	Stephen Mather convinces the Department of the Interior to create the National Park Service.

The Father of National Parks

Often considered the father of the US national park system, Scottish-born John Muir (1838–1914) was an eloquent writer, naturalist and arguably the greatest defender of wilderness areas in the late-19th century. His writings were pivotal in the creation not just of Yosemite, but of Sequoia, Mt Rainier, Petrified Forest and Grand Canyon National Parks. Famously – but unsuccessfully – Muir fought to save Yosemite's Hetch Hetchy Valley, which he believed rivaled Yosemite Valley in beauty and grandeur. Although he couldn't stop the damming of the river, his writings on the issue cemented the now widely held belief that America's national parks should remain as close as possible to their natural state.

Yosemite Valley, and the nearby Mariposa Grove of giant sequoias, under the control of California. Although it wasn't a national park, it was the first time *any* government had mandated the protection of a natural area for public use.

Birth of a National Park

Four years later, a group of men bankrolled by Northern Pacific Railroad headed into the Wyoming wilderness to investigate reports of thermal pools and geysers. Among their discoveries were the Great Fountain Geyser and another geyser they would name Old Faithful. Soon, lobbyists at Northern Pacific, with their eyes on tourist dollars, rallied alongside conservationists for a public park like Yosemite. In 1872 President Ulysses S Grant signed the landmark Yellowstone National Park Act, creating the country's first national park.

Meanwhile, in Yosemite, the famed naturalist John Muir lamented the destruction that logging companies, miners and sheep – which he famously deemed 'hoofed locusts' – were wreaking upon the park. In 1890 Yosemite became the country's second national park, but it wasn't until 1905 that Muir convinced Congress to expand the boundaries to include all of Yosemite Valley and the Mariposa Grove.

Over the next 25 years, presidents signed off on six more national parks, and the momentum to set aside areas for protection became irreversible.

Mather & the National Park Service

Still, there existed no effective protection or management of the new parks until the creation of the National Park Service (NPS) in 1916. The NPS was the brainchild of an industrialist and conservationist named Stephen Mather, who convinced the Department of the Interior that a single governing body was precisely what the parks needed. When President Woodrow Wilson signed the National Park Service Act into law, Mather became the first director.

Mather believed that the best way to promote and improve the parks was to get people into them. A public relations guru, Mather encouraged park superintendents to run pub-

1923	**1926**	**1933**
Yosemite's Hetch Hetchy Valley is dammed, the first shot in a continuing battle between conservationists and developers.	Yellowstone's last wolves are killed in the federal predator control program, which also targeted mountain lions, bears and coyotes.	FDR creates the Civilian Conservation Corps; CCC workers improve infrastructure in national parks and plant over 3 billion trees.

licity campaigns, created the park ranger system, initiated campfire talks and opened the first park museums. His efforts – always coupled with media outreach – were so successful that by 1928 he had tripled the number of park visitors to three million.

While Mather was extremely successful in developing the parks, some felt he'd gone too far. Conservation groups such as the National Parks Association and the Sierra Club felt that Mather's emphasis on development came at the expense of the parks themselves. Mather's successor and protégé, Horace Albright, partially addressed these concerns by creating a national wildlife division within the NPS.

FDR & the CCC

With the Great Depression, the parks went through significant changes. President Franklin Delano Roosevelt (FDR) created the Civilian Conservation Corps (CCC) and put thousands of young men to work improving national park roads, visitors' shelters, campsites and trails. During his presidency, FDR also created Joshua Tree, Capitol Reef, and Channel Islands National Monuments (all of which would become national parks), and Olympic, Kings Canyon, Everglades and Great Smoky Mountains National Parks.

With the beginning of WWII, the country's greatest public relief program came to an end, CCC workers went off to war, and the national park budget was slashed. Simultaneously, postwar prosperity allowed more Americans to travel – and hordes of them headed to the parks. By 1950 some 32 million people visited America's national parks. Within five years the number topped 60 million.

Mission 66

The number of travelers descending on the parks puts tremendous pressure on them. In 1956 NPS Director Conrad Wirth created Mission 66, a 10-year plan to improve park

Theodore Roosevelt: The Conservation President

As part of a 1903 campaign tour, President Theodore Roosevelt spent two weeks exploring Yellowstone and three nights camping out with John Muir in Yosemite. But the greatest legacy of that trip arose from time spent at the Grand Canyon. Upon seeing the canyon for the first time, Roosevelt famously opined that the mystical natural wonder could not be improved by any human intervention – it should be left exactly as it was. A nascent conservationist movement had just gained an influential new member.

Muir may have provided the philosophical underpinnings of the national parks, but it was Roosevelt who transformed the vision into reality. An avid hunter, birder, far-sighted thinker and lover of the outdoors, Roosevelt's time out West – before he became president – profoundly shaped his life and legacy. By the time he left office in 1909, he had signed off on five national parks, 18 national monuments, 51 federal bird sanctuaries and 100 million acres of national forest.

1934
The Everglades and Great Smoky Mountains National Parks are created just 15 days apart at the height of the Great Depression.

1941–49
Ansel Adams photographs every national park in the US, bar the Everglades, for the NPS.

1956–66
Mission 66 improves park facilities and creates the first national park visitor centers.

The Antiquities Act, National Monuments & Other NPS Sites

In 1906 Congress passed the Antiquities Act, giving the president the authority to protect public land by designating it a National Monument. It was originally designed to protect Native American archaeological sites out West, but Theodore Roosevelt realized he could use the Act to protect any tract of land for any reason, and without opposition from lobbyists or political opponents in Congress.

In 2022 there were 129 national monuments. More get designated every year, while others change status. Most are administered by the NPS. Other sites under NPS jurisdiction include those named as National Historic Sites and Parks, National Memorials, National Parkways, National Seashores, National Recreation Areas and National Preserves, which are like parks, except that fossil-fuel extraction and sport hunting are permitted. The NPS currently administers over 400 natural and historic sites, including 63 national parks.

infrastructure and dramatically increase visitors' services. The plan established the first park visitor centers, more staff and improved facilities. Over the course of Mission 66, Congress also added more than 50 new protected areas to the national park system.

In 1964 George Hartzog succeeded Wirth as director of the NPS and continued with new acquisitions. During his tenure nearly 70 new parks would come under the jurisdiction of the NPS. In 1972 President Nixon replaced Hartzog with his own appointee, and expansions to the park service were halted.

Doubling Down

Little was added to the national parks system until 1980, when President Carter signed the Alaska National Interest Lands Conservation Act into law. The landmark legislation instantly protected over 80 million acres and doubled the amount of land under control of the national parks, with 10 new national parks and monuments created in the process. Although controversial in Alaska, the move has been widely heralded as one of the greatest conservation measures in US history.

Recent Times

Since Yellowstone was created in 1872, the national park system has grown to encompass over 400 sites and more than 84 million acres. The parks today protect many of the continent's most sensitive ecosystems, some of the world's most remarkable landscapes and America's most important historical and cultural landmarks. According to the National Park Service, the total number of visitors to US national parks between 1904 and 2021 was around 15.4 billion. They are the country's greatest treasure.

1980
The Alaska National Interest Lands Conservation Act doubles the amount of land under NPS control.

1995
Gray wolves are reintroduced to Yellowstone nearly 70 years after disappearing from the park ecosystem.

2011
A proposed ban on the sale of plastic water bottles in the Grand Canyon is blocked after Coca-Cola, an NPS donor, expresses displeasure.

Despite a steady increase in visitation, however, the parks still face a variety of threats and obstacles, including loss of biodiversity, declining air and water quality, climate disruption and insufficient funding. In 2011 the NPS released a Call to Action: an initiative to help the service prepare for its second century, with aims such as reducing greenhouse gas emissions by 20%, increasing community involvement and continuing to raise awareness for the parks among all Americans.

Hot Topics

While conservationists, policy makers and the NPS debate how to best protect the parks, nearly everyone agrees the parks need money – except, it seems, for Congress. With budget cuts and obstructionist gridlock becoming increasingly the norm in Washington, the NPS has begun to turn to private donors and corporate sponsorships in order to make up for the federal shortfall.

System-wide challenges are not the only matters garnering national attention. Congestion, crowds and vehicles remain a constant source of concern, and more and more parks are introducing free shuttles to combat traffic and reduce air pollution. And from the ongoing debate about unsustainable visitor numbers in the Great Smoky Mountains National Park to water quality and the plague of invasive species in the Everglades, there are plenty of other park-specific issues to be dealt with.

National Monuments of Florida & the South

Birmingham Civil Rights, Alabama
Camp Nelson, Kentucky
Castillo de San Marcos, Florida
Fort Frederica, Georgia
Fort Pulaski, Georgia
Freedom Riders, Alabama
Medgar & Myrlie Evers Home, Mississippi
Mill Springs Battlefield, Kentucky
Poverty Point, Louisiana
Russell Cave, Alabama

2016
The National Park Service celebrates the 100th anniversary of its founding.

2017
Park visitation reaches an all-time high, with 330.97 million visitors over the course of the year.

2020
At the height of the COVID-19 pandemic park visitor numbers fall to 237 million (the lowest since 1980), rebounding to 297.1 million in 2021.

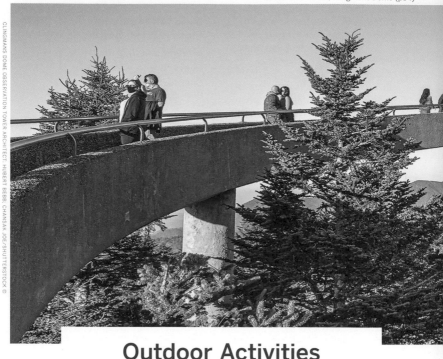

CLINGMANS DOME OBSERVATION TOWER ARCHITECT: HUBERT BEBB, CHANSAK JOE/SHUTTERSTOCK ©

Outdoor Activities

We've yet to meet someone visiting a national park so they can hang around indoors. The outdoors is what the parks are all about, and getting out usually means getting active. With environments ranging from the subtropics of the Everglades to the high trails and rafting rivers of the Great Smoky Mountains, the possibilities can seem endless.

Hiking

Nothing encapsulates the spirit of the national parks like hiking. Thousands of miles of trails crisscross the parks, offering access to their most scenic mountain passes, highest water-falls, deepest canyons and quietest corners. Trails run the gamut of accessibility, from the boardwalks of the Everglades wetlands to the summit hikes of the Great Smoky Mountains.

Regardless of the style of the trail, you'll find that exploring on foot generally offers the best park experience. The relatively slow pace of walking brings you into closer contact with the wildlife, and allows you to appreciate the way different perspectives and the day's shifting light can alter the scenery. The satisfaction gained from completing a hike is also a worthy reward; it's one thing to admire from afar the summit of Clingmans Dome in the Great Smoky Mountains, it's another to work up a sweat hiking all the way to the top.

Detailed trail descriptions and maps are readily available at visitor centers in every park, and they will complement this guide well. Know your limitations, know the route you plan to take and pace yourself.

Backpacking

There are plenty of amazing day hikes to choose from in the park system, but if you want the full experience, head out into the wilderness on an overnight trip. The claim that 99% of park visitors never make it into the backcountry may not be true everywhere, but you will unquestionably see far fewer people and witness exponentially more magic the further from a road you go. Backcountry campgrounds are also much more likely to have openings than park lodges and car campgrounds (which fill up months in advance), making accommodations less of a headache.

Even if you have no backpacking experience, don't consider it out of reach. Most national parks have at least a few backcountry campgrounds within a couple of hours' walk of a trailhead, making them excellent options for first-time backpackers. You will need gear, however: an appropriate backpack, tent, sleeping bag and pad, headlamp, stove and food are all essential.

Familiarize yourself with the park rules and backcountry ethics before heading out. You will need a permit; if you have your heart set on a famous excursion, apply well in advance online. Most park visitor centers have a backcountry desk, where you can apply for walk-in permits, get trail information, learn about wildlife (bear canisters are generally required in bear country) and check conditions. Before hitting the trail, learn about low-impact camping principles at Leave No Trace (www.lnt.org).

★ **Classic Short Hikes**

Alum Cave Bluffs, Great Smoky Mountains

Ramsey Cascades, Great Smoky Mountains

Oakridge Trail, Congaree

Mt LeConte, Great Smoky Mountains

Anhinga Trail, Everglades (pictured)

Preparation & Safety

Walks can be as short or long as you like, but remember this when planning: be prepared. The wilderness may be unlike anything you have ever experienced, and designating certain parcels as 'national parks' has not tamed it.

The weather can be extraordinary in its unpredictability and sheer force. The summer sun is blazing hot, sudden thunderstorms can drop enough water in 10 minutes to create deadly flash floods, snow can fall at any time of year above tree lines, while ferocious wind storms can rip or blow away your poorly staked tent.

No matter where you are, water should be the number one item on your packing checklist – always carry more than you think you'll need. If you're doing any backpacking, make sure you have a way to purify water, and check with rangers ahead of time about the availability of water along the trail.

After the elements, getting lost is the next major concern. Most day hikes are well signed and visitors are numerous, but you should always take some sort of map. If you plan on going into the backcountry, definitely take a topographic (topo) map and a compass. You can pick up detailed maps in most visitor centers; National Geographic's *Trails Illustrated* series is generally excellent.

At lower elevations and in desert parks, always inquire about ticks, poison oak, poison ivy and rattlesnakes before heading out. Most day hikes are on well-maintained trails, but it's good to know what's out there.

And all hikers, solo or not, should always remember the golden rule: let someone know where you are going and how long you plan to be gone.

Kayaking, Canoeing & Rafting

The waterways of the **Everglades** rank among the best kayaking destinations anywhere in the US – there are infinite trails, plenty of wildlife to keep you company, and numerous highly professional operators to get you out on the water.

In the northern Everglades paddlers have seemingly endless options, with many Everglades channels to choose from and the 10,000 Islands lying just offshore. **Wilderness Waterway**, a 99-mile route between Everglades City and Flamingo, is the longest canoe trail in the area. Most islands are fringed by narrow beaches with pure, white sand. The water is brackish and usually very shallow, but the scenery is captivating in its own right. You can camp on your own island for up to a week.

In the southern Everglades there are plenty of push-off points, all with names that sound like they come from Frodo's map to Mordor in *The Lord of the Rings*, including Hell's Bay, the Nightmare, Snake Bight and Graveyard Creek. Trails include **Nine Mile Pond** (3- or 5.2-mile loop), **Noble Hammock** (2 miles return), **Hell's Bay** (5.5 miles one way), **West Lake**

(7.7 miles one way), Mud Lake (7 miles return) and **Bear Lake** (11.5 miles one way).

Elsewhere, **Cedar Creek** (Congaree) meanders through 27 miles of wilderness and is good for kayaking or canoeing, while **Green River** cuts a beautiful canoeable path through Mammoth Cave National Park.

Options are limited for paddling in the Great Smoky Mountains because of the park's shallow, rock-filled streams. One exception is **Fontana Lake** on the southern edge of the park, west of Bryson City. Framed by forest-covered slopes, the 29-mile-long lake, with its deep blue waters, is a lovely spot for a paddle.

Rafting in the Great Smokys is an altogether different proposition. One of the top spots in the southeast for white-water rafting is along the **Pigeon River**, just northeast of the park. Local outfitters run adrenaline-fueled trips along the Upper Pigeon, with quieter family-friendly trips best enjoyed along the Lower Pigeon.

> ### So Much to Do...
>
> For those that want to try it all, here's some more fodder for fun:
>
> **Soaking** Submerge your sore muscles in thermal waters at Hot Springs, along the Appalachian Trail.
>
> **Stargazing** The night sky over Dry Tortugas is truly a wonder to behold.
>
> **Caving** Join a subterranean tour at Mammoth Cave.
>
> **Windsurfing** Surf the breeze around Convoy Point, or with Miami as a backdrop, at Biscayne.

Boat Tours & Snorkeling

Boat trips exploring the vast **Everglades** are *de rigueur* in the dry season. The best selection of boat tours operates in the northern Everglades, from along the Tamiami Trail, Everglades City and out into the 10,000 Islands, where if you're lucky you may see dolphins springing up beside your craft.

Only 5% of **Biscayne**, Florida's largest stretch of undeveloped Atlantic coastline, is land – glass-bottom boats and snorkeling tours are obligatory to check out the coral reefs offshore. Biscayne is a fantastic place to explore, guided by the multisite **Maritime Heritage Trail**. Wherever you go, there's plenty to see – Biscayne National Park has shipwrecks, more than 500 kinds of fish (including parrotfish, angelfish, wrasses and butterfly fish) as well as sea cucumbers and the gloriously named Christmas tree worm.

If you're prepared to leave the continental US by boat or seaplane, the **Dry Tortugas** is certainly the best option for snorkeling and diving in sapphire-blue waters off Florida's Gulf Coast. Only 1% of the park (about 143 acres out of 70 sq miles) consists of dry land, with much of the park's allure lying under the water. The marine life is quite rich here, with the opportunity to see tarpon, sizable groupers and lots of colorful coral and smaller tropical fish, plus the odd sea turtle.

Cycling & Mountain Biking

As a general rule, expect more options for two-wheeled fun just outside park boundaries. There are, however, some exceptions. For example, bicycles are allowed on park roads in the **Great Smoky Mountains**. On the downside, cycling within national parks, especially one as popular as Great Smoky, can be challenging due to steep grades and heavy traffic, as anyone who's been grazed by an RV mirror knows.

Mountain biking on trails is largely prohibited in national parks, but some parks have dirt roads that substitute, and there are several gravel roads in the Great Smoky Mountains.

★ Classic Long Hikes

Appalachian Trail

Charlies Bunion & Kephart Loop, Great Smoky Mountains (pictured)

Grandfather Mountain, Blue Ridge Parkway

Swimming

As river rats the world over will attest, nothing beats dipping into a swimming hole and drip-drying on a rock in the sun. But be careful – every year swimmers drown in national park rivers. Always check with visitor centers about danger spots and the safest places to swim. Unless you're certain about the currents, swim only where others are swimming.

In the Great Smoky Mountains, visitors are discouraged from swimming or even wading in streams and natural pools around the park. Currents are strong and unseen obstacles can lead to bad falls, or getting your legs pinned while the water forces you under the surface. Drowning is one of the leading causes of death in the park.

Swimming is not allowed in the Everglades, not least because you never quite know what you'll be sharing the water with...

Fishing

For many, the idea of heading to the national parks without a fishing rod is ludicrous. The **Great Smoky Mountains** has exceptional fishing for trout and bass.

Wherever you fish, read up on local regulations. Fishing permits are always required, and those caught fishing without one will be fined. (Children under 15 are generally not required to have a license.) Some waters, including many streams and rivers, are catch-and-release only, and sometimes bait-fishing is prohibited. Certain native fish, such as bull trout, kokanee salmon and wild steelhead, are often protected, and anglers in possession of these can be heavily fined. The best place to check regulations is online: read the NPS's details on the parks at www.nps.gov and refer to each respective state's Department of Fish and Game website.

Horseback Riding

Our most time-tested form of transport still makes for a wonderful way to experience the great outdoors.

Horseback riding is possible in the **Great Smoky Mountains**, where over 550 miles of trails are open to horses. The park has three stables that open between mid-March and mid-November. There's everything from one-hour to four-hour rides, starting at around $35 per hour.

Egrets

FLORIDASTOCK/SHUTTERSTOCK ©

Flora & Fauna

Since the 19th century America's national parks have played a critical role in bringing many signature US species – among them bison, elk, wolf, mountain lion and grizzly bear – back from the brink of extinction. More recently, Florida has become a front line for the battle to save other iconic species, including the Florida panther and the American crocodile.

Land Mammals

Despite being one of the most overdeveloped states in the US, Florida has a surprising range of wildlife species, and some of these spill over into other southern states.

Florida Panther

The critically endangered Florida panther, the state's official animal, was in deep trouble as recently as the early 1990s, with as few as 10 (and no more than 30) left in the wild. East of the Mississippi there were, and remain, no other known populations of mountain lions (also known as cougars, pumas and, in Florida, the Florida panther). Those that did inhabit southwestern Florida had already developed a number of genetic problems (including heart defects) that came from close inbreeding. In the mid-1990s scientists brought in eight female mountain lions from Texas. The population in Florida began to grow, the genetic flaws began to disappear and estimates of the number of Florida panthers now range between 130 and 200. In November 2016 a female panther became the first of her kind to cross the Caloosahatchee River; although males had crossed the river before, the female, who soon had cubs, represented an important milestone for the species.

Many challenges remain, however. As usual, humans have been the culprits behind the threat to this predator. Widespread habitat reduction (ie the arrival of big subdivisions) is the major cause of concern. Breeding units (one male and two to five females) require about 200 sq miles, and that often puts panthers in the way of one of Florida's most dangerous beasts: drivers. Some 31 panthers were killed by cars in 2016, with 26, 24 and 23 killed in the following three years. Underpasses have been critical in reducing their fatalities. Planned major new roads, including one between Orlando and Naples, will cut through habitat considered essential if the Florida panther population is to grow.

Rather magnificent golden-brown hunting cats, Florida panthers are extremely elusive and only inhabit 5% of their historic range. They're found in the northern Everglades region, with denser concentrations in Big Cypress National Preserve and Florida Panther National Wildlife Refuge. Sightings are also possible in Corkscrew Swamp Sanctuary. To learn more about the battle to save the panther, read *Cat Tale* (2020), by Craig Pittman.

Black Bears

Black bears, which are sometimes brown- or cinnamon-colored, roam montane and subalpine forests throughout the country.

Florida black bears have recovered to a population of around 3000 to 4000, but as their forests diminish, bears are occasionally seen traipsing through suburbs in northern Florida. There are seven known populations in Florida, including in Ocala National Forest, Big Cypress National Preserve and Apalachicola National Forest, although they're also nearby in Georgia, Alabama and Mississippi, and in the Great Smoky Mountains (which has a population of around 1500). Naples Zoo also has captive black bears.

Black bears are very adaptable and in some places have become so accustomed to humans that they regularly roam campgrounds and break into cars at night for food. Make sure you store your food and trash properly, and use a bear canister if you plan on backpacking.

Coyotes & Wolves

Coyotes are common in many of the parks, but you're far more likely to hear them than see them. Listening to them howl at night as you doze off to sleep is an eerie yet wonderful experience. Although they are ostensibly native to the American West, the adaptable coyote has been spotted across Florida, appearing as far south as the Florida Keys.

The critically endangered red wolf once roamed the bottomlands, marshes and flooded forests of the American eastern seaboard, particularly in the southeast. Due to hunting and habitat loss the red wolf was almost wiped out, but a breeding population has been established at the St Vincent National Wildlife Refuge, located off the Panhandle coast.

Marine Mammals

Florida's coastal waters are home to 21 species of dolphins and whales. By far the most common is the bottlenose dolphin, which is highly social, extremely intelligent and frequently encountered around the entire peninsula.

The North Atlantic population of about 300 right whales comes to winter calving grounds off the Atlantic Coast near Jacksonville. These giant animals can be more than 50ft long, and are the most endangered species of whale.

River otters are commonly seen in the waterways of the Everglades. Winter is also the season for manatees, which seek out Florida's warm-water springs and power-plant discharge canals, beginning in November.

Birds

Nearly 500 avian species have been documented in Florida, including some of the world's most magnificent migratory waterbirds: ibis, egrets, great blue herons, white pelicans and whooping cranes. Completed in 2006, the Great Florida Birding Trail (www.floridabirdingtrail.com) runs for 2000 miles and includes nearly 500 bird-watching sites.

Nearly 350 species spend time in the Everglades, Florida's prime bird-watching spot, including 16 different wading birds and dozens of terns, gulls and other shorebirds.

About 5000 nonmigratory sandhill cranes are joined by 25,000 migratory cousins each winter. White whooping cranes – at up to 5ft they are the tallest bird in North America – are nearly extinct. About 100 winter on Florida's Gulf Coast near Homosassa.

The state has more than 1000 mated pairs of bald eagles, the most in the southern US, and peregrine falcons, which can dive at speeds of up to 150mph, migrate through in spring and fall.

Florida's Manatees

It's hard to believe Florida's West Indian manatees were ever mistaken for mermaids, but it's easy to see their attraction: these gentle, curious, colossal mammals are as sweetly lovable as 10ft, 1500lb teddy bears. Solitary and playful, they have been known to 'surf' waves, and every winter, from November to March, they migrate into the warmer waters of Florida's freshwater estuaries, rivers and springs.

Florida residents for more than 45 million years, these shy herbivores have absolutely no defenses except their size, and they don't do much, spending most of each day resting and eating 10% of their body weight in food. Rarely moving faster than a languid saunter, manatees even reproduce slowly; females birth one calf every two to five years. The exception to their docility? Mating. Males are notorious for their aggressive sex drive.

Florida's manatees have been under some form of protection since 1893, and they were included in the first federal endangered species list in 1967. Manatees were once hunted for their meat, and today collisions with boats are a leading cause of manatee deaths – propeller scars are so ubiquitous among the living that they are the chief identifying tool of scientists. At the time of writing there were roughly 6000 manatees left in the state.

Amphibians & Reptiles

Frogs, toads and salamanders thrive in and around streams, rivers and lakes in several of the parks. With 24 species of salamanders, the Great Smoky Mountains is often deemed the salamander capital of the world.

Boasting an estimated 184 species, Florida has the nation's largest collection of reptiles and amphibians. Unfortunately, uninvited guests add to their numbers regularly, many establishing themselves after being released by pet owners. Some of the more dangerous, problematic and invasive species include Burmese pythons, black and green iguanas and Nile monitor lizards.

The American alligator is Florida's poster species, and they are ubiquitous in Central and South Florida. South Florida is also home to the only North American population of American crocodile. Florida's crocs number around 1500; they prefer saltwater. The Everglades is also home to 16 turtle and tortoise species.

Florida has 44 species of snake (20 of which are in the Everglades), although only six species are poisonous, and only four of those are common. Of the baddies, three are rattlesnakes (diamondback, pygmy and canebrake), and there are copperheads, cottonmouths and coral snakes. Fortunately most visitors will never even see one.

Sea Turtles

Most sea-turtle nesting in the continental US occurs in Florida. Predominantly three species create more than 80,000 nests annually, mostly on southern Atlantic Coast beaches but extending to all Gulf Coast beaches. Most are loggerhead, with far fewer green and leatherback turtles. Historically hawksbill and Kemp's ridley turtles were also present in numbers as well. The leatherback is the largest, attaining 10ft and 2000lb in size. All five species are endangered or threatened.

During the May-to-October nesting season, sea turtles deposit from 80 to 120 eggs in each nest. The eggs incubate for about two months, then the hatchlings emerge all at once and make for the ocean. Contrary to myth, hatchlings don't need the moon to find their way to the sea. However, they can become hopelessly confused by artificial lights and noisy human audiences. For the best, least-disruptive experience, join a sanctioned turtle watch; for details, visit www.myfwc.com/seaturtle, then click on 'Sea Turtle Viewing Opportunities.'

Trees & Plants of Florida

What Florida lacks in topographical variety, it more than makes up for in plant diversity. The varied nature of the peninsula's flora, including more than 4000 species of plants, is unmatched in the continental US. Florida contains the southern extent of temperate ecosystems and the northern extent of tropical ones, which blend and merge in a bewildering, fluid taxonomy of environments. Interestingly, most of the world at this latitude is desert, which Florida definitely is not.

Wetlands & Swamps

It takes a special kind of plant to thrive in the humid, waterlogged, sometimes-salty marshes, sloughs, swales, seeps, basins, marl prairies and swamps of Florida, and several hundred specialized native plants have evolved to do so. Much of the Everglades is dominated by vast expanses of saw grass, which is actually a sedge with fine toothlike edges that can reach 10ft high. South Florida is a symphony of sedges, grasses and rushes. These hardy water-tolerant species provide abundant seeds to feed birds and animals, protect fish in shallow water, and pad wetlands for birds and alligators.

The strangest plants are the submerged and immersed species that grow in, under and out of the water. Free-floating species include bladderwort and coontail, a species that lives, flowers and is pollinated entirely underwater. Florida's swamps are abundant with rooted plants with floating leaves, including the pretty American lotus, water lilies and spatterdock. Another common immersed plant, bur marigolds, can paint whole prairies yellow.

Another dramatic, beautiful tree in Florida's swamps is the bald cypress, the most flood-tolerant tree. It can grow 150ft tall, with buttressed, wide trunks and roots with 'knees' that poke above the drenched soil. Cypress domes are a particular type of swamp that arise when a watery depression occurs in a pine flatwood.

Forests, Scrubs & Flatwoods

Florida's northern forests, particularly in the Panhandle, are an epicenter of plant and animal biodiversity, just as much as its southern swamps. Here the continent's temperate forests of hickory, elm, ash, maple, magnolia and locust trees combine with the pine, gum and oak trees that are common throughout Florida, along with the saw grass, cypress and cabbage palms of southern Florida. The wet but temperate Apalachicola forest supports 40 kinds of trees and more insect species than scientists can count.

Mangroves & Coastal Dunes

Plenty of southern Florida's coastline is covered in mangroves. Mangroves are not a single species; the name refers to all tropical trees and shrubs that have adapted to loose wet soil, saltwater and periodic root submergence, usually between high and low tides. Mangroves have also developed 'live birth,' germinating their seeds while they're still attached to the parent tree. Of more than 50 species of mangroves worldwide, only three predominate in Florida: red, black and white.

Ghost Hunters

Florida has more species of orchids than any other state in the US, and orchids are themselves the largest family of flowering plants in the world, with perhaps 25,000 species. The Florida orchid that inspires the most intense devotion is the rare ghost orchid.

This bizarre epiphytic flower has no leaves and usually only one bloom, which is deathly white with two long, thin drooping petals that curl like a handlebar mustache. The ghost orchid is pollinated in the dead of night by the giant sphinx moth, which is the only insect with a proboscis long enough to reach down the ghost orchid's 5in-long nectar spur.

The exact locations of ghost orchids are kept secret for fear of poachers, who, as made clear in Susan Orlean's book *The Orchid Thief* (1998), are a real threat to their survival.

To learn more visit Sarasota's Marie Selby Botanical Gardens.

Mangroves play a vital role on the peninsula, and their destruction usually sets off a domino effect of ecological damage. Mangroves stabilize coastal land, trapping sand, silt and sediment; as this builds up, new land is created, which ironically strangles the mangroves themselves. Mangroves mitigate the storm surge and damaging winds of hurricanes, and anchor tidal and estuary communities, providing vital wildlife habitats.

Trees & Plants of the Great Smoky Mountains

The Great Smoky Mountains boast a staggering variety of plant life, with a greater diversity of flora than any other place in North America. This national park is home to around 100 native tree species and more than 1500 flowering plants. Much of its diversity is due to its wide variations in geography and elevation (from 875ft to more than 6600ft), with both southern and northern species present. The park's abundant rainfall and high humidity in the warmer months also provides ideal growing conditions.

Hemlock Forest

Hemlock forests dominate at lower elevations (below 4000ft) in moist areas, across shaded slopes and along streams. Around 136 sq miles of the park are covered by hemlock forests. These evergreen trees were saved from felling as they weren't commercially valued by lumber companies. As a result some of the oldest and largest trees in the park are eastern hemlocks. They've been called the 'redwoods of the east,' and can grow to more than 150ft tall and up to 10ft in diameter. Some specimens in the park are more than

A Chinese Connection

The Great Smoky Mountains are home to over 17,000 identified plant and animal species. This ancient ecoregion shares a surprisingly similar taxonomic makeup with southwestern China – including such plant genera as magnolia, hickory, sassafras and ginseng.

500 years old, although invasive species like the non-native woolly adelgid insect are a major threat for hemlocks.

Pine & Oak Forest

In the mountains up to about 4500ft, where the slopes are dry and exposed, you can expect to find forests dominated by pine and oak trees. These types of forests are more common on the west side of the park. Thickets of mountain laurel and stands of rhododendron grow well here, as do flowering dogwood trees, galax, yellow poplars and hickory. Of the park's 11 species of oak and five species of pine, the most commonly found trees are scarlet oak, chestnut oak, black oak, Table Mountain pine, Virginia pine and pitch pine. Forest fires are not uncommon in these habitats and can be necessary for some species' reproduction and forest regeneration.

Cove Hardwood Forest

In Appalachian parlance, coves are sheltered valleys with deep, fertile soil. Here are found the most botanically diverse forests of the Smoky Mountains, which grow on slopes up to 4500ft. You'll find tulip tree, yellow buckeye, sugar maple, black cherry, magnolia, yellow birch and Carolina silverbell among dozens of other species. Wildflowers are also profuse in these forests, and the fall colors are dazzling. Those regions passed over by loggers boast trees of record size. One of the best places to see these forests for yourself is along the Ramsey Cascades Trail, or the shorter Cove Hardwood Nature Trail at Chimneys Picnic Area off Newfound Gap Rd.

Northern Hardwood Forest

Growing at elevations of 4500ft to 6000ft, these broad-leaved forests have a decidedly northern feel, akin to the wooded areas of New England and the Great Lakes region. In these forests you'll find predominantly American beech and yellow birch in the canopy, along with mountain maple, white basswood, yellow buckeye and pin cherry. Around 44 sq miles of northern hardwood forest is old-growth. The Smokies are also known for their beech gaps, where stands of American beech trees take over and monopolize high mountain gaps. Look for them on south-facing slopes along the high ridges, such as along the road up Clingmans Dome, where the gaps interrupt spruce-fir forest at regular intervals.

Chimney Tops trail, Great Smokey Mountains National Park (p60)

WEIDMAN PHOTOGRAPHY/SHUTTERSTOCK ©

Conservation

Protecting the national parks has been a challenge since their 19th-century beginnings. Thanks to the efforts of passionate individuals, the parks now safeguard some of the greatest natural treasures on the planet. But they face new, often concurrent, threats. Climate change, invasive species, overdevelopment and poor water management all jeopardize national parks today.

Climate Change & Invasive Species

Climate change poses a significant threat to the health of the national park network's diverse ecosystems, whether in the form of melting glaciers or bigger and more destructive wildfires in parks like the Great Smoky Mountains and surrounding areas.

Nowhere in the US does global warming matter more than in the low-lying Florida Keys. In December 2019 a long-awaited report quantified the cost of elevating 300 miles of county roads across the Keys; the details were frightening. The report took a representative sample of a populated 3-mile road at the southern end of Sugarloaf Key, an island 15 miles east of Key West. To elevate the road 1.3ft to a height where it could be dry and open year-round would cost $75 million; by 2060 the cost would be $181 million.

Invasive species also pose a severe threat to the national parks. In the Southern Appalachians, a non-native insect called the woolly adelgid is decimating eastern hemlock forests. In the Great Smoky Mountains National Park, where the insect was discovered in 2003, trees are already beginning to die. In Shenandoah, Virginia, where the insect has been present since 1980, nearly 95% of hemlocks have perished.

And the Everglades is awash in invasive species, most famously the Burmese python, which is eating its way through the park's wildlife.

Human Impact

Aside from the effect visitors have on the parks, humans are putting immense pressure on many locations by operating high-impact businesses outside park boundaries. The Great Smoky Mountains is one of a number of parks affected by emissions from coal-fired power plants, which drift over parks and contaminate the air.

But it's Florida that's the unfortunate poster child for human impact upon the natural world, which is the inevitable result of its long love affair with land development, population growth and tourism. The complex, intertwined environmental consequences include erosion of wetlands, depletion of the aquifer, rampant pollution (particularly of waters), widespread habitat destruction and invasive and endangered species.

The state has enacted several significant conservation efforts. In 2000 it passed the Florida Forever Act, which the state claims is the nation's largest public land acquisition program. By 2020 the program had purchased nearly one million acres for public protection and manages 10 times that amount of land for conservation.

Even so, residential development continues almost unabated. The Miami–Fort Lauderdale–West Palm Beach corridor (the USA's fourth-largest urban area) is, as developers say, 'built out,' so they have begun targeting the Panhandle and Central Florida. Most concerning of all, it is estimated that the state's population will have doubled between 2006 and 2060.

Water Management

More than half of Florida's lakes have elevated levels of algae, which leads to frequent toxic blooms that wipe out local wildlife. Though industrial pollution has been curtailed, pollution from residential development (sewage, fertilizer runoff) more than compensates. This distresses Florida's freshwater springs, which can turn murky and undrinkable, while pumping groundwater is causing an increase in sinkholes. Such direct consequences of overdevelopment are worrying signs that the state's waterways may be facing longer-term trouble.

In 2000 the US Congress passed the multibillion-dollar Comprehensive Everglades Restoration Plan and the associated Central Everglades Planning Project. Unfortunately, implementation of the latter plan has been problematic due to a lack of approval from federal agencies such as the Army Corps of Engineers.

Visiting National Parks Sustainably

Park visitors can make a positive impact by traveling sustainably and getting involved with park associations. Whenever you can, ride park shuttles instead of driving your car. Avoid high-impact park activities such as airboating in the Everglades, and prevent erosion by always staying on trails. If you're backpacking, use biodegradable soaps (or skip them altogether) and follow the principles of Leave No Trace (www.lnt.org).

Nearly every national park has an associated foundation or a nonprofit that supports its parent park. The National Parks Conservation Association (www.npca.org) covers all of the parks. Since 1919 this nonprofit organization has been protecting and preserving America's national parks through research, advocacy and education.

MIA2YOU/SHUTTERSTOCK ©

★ **Did you know?**

More than 200 national parks and monuments in the US contain at least one endangered species.

BOTTOM LEFT: EHRLIF, SHUTTERSTOCK ©; BOTTOM RIGHT, HEIKO K EPA/SHUTTERSTOCK ©

Top: Highway to Key West; Bottom left: Dead trees, Great Smoky Mountains; Bottom right: Burmese python (p109), Everglades

Intracoastal Waterway, Jacksonville Beach, Florida

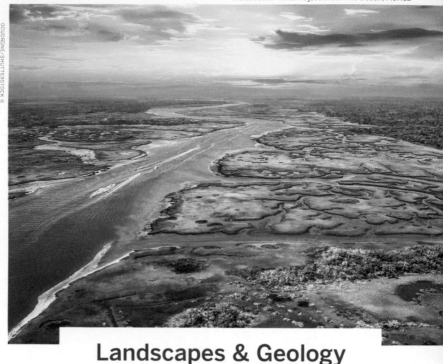

OCUDIGNE/SHUTTERSTOCK ©

Landscapes & Geology

*Tectonic collisions, glaciation, volcanic eruptions, erosion –
the forces of nature and time have worked wonders on the
continent, and in few places is that geological history more
beautifully evident than in the national parks of Florida and
the South. Each park tells its own ancient story through
landscapes that are as unique as they are complex.*

Florida

Florida is many things, but elevated it is decidedly not. The state's highest point, the
Florida Panhandle's Britton Hill, has to stretch to reach 350ft, which isn't half as tall as the
buildings of downtown Miami. This makes Florida officially the nation's flattest state. With
an average elevation of only 6ft, the Everglades is actually an expansive wetland atop an
ancient seabed, with a tremendous variety of coastal and marine ecosystems.

Florida is the US state with the longest coastline (apart from Alaska), and is 22nd in
total area (58,560 sq miles). However, more than 4000 of those square miles are water;
lakes and springs pepper the map like bullet holes in a road sign. The shotgun-sized hole
in the south is Lake Okeechobee, one of the USA's largest freshwater lakes. It might sound

Fish sheltering under coral, Florida Keys

DURDEN IMAGES/SHUTTERSTOCK ©

impressive, but the bottom of the lake is only a few feet above sea level – it's so shallow you can practically wade across.

Every year Lake Okeechobee ever so gently floods the southern tip of the peninsula. Or it tries to – canals divert much of the flow either to irrigation fields or to Florida's bracketing major bodies of water: the Gulf of Mexico and the Atlantic Ocean. But were the water to follow the natural lay of the land, it would flow downwards: from its center, the state of Florida inclines about 6in every 6 miles until, finally, the peninsula can't keep its head above water anymore. What was an unelevated plain peters out into the 10,000 Islands and the Florida Keys, which end with a flourish in the Gulf of Mexico. Key West, the last in the chain, is the southernmost point in the continental US.

South Florida

When the waters of Okeechobee flood the South Florida plain, they interact with the local grasslands and limestone to create a wilderness unlike any other: the Everglades. They also fill up the freshwater aquifers that are required for maintaining human habitation in the ever-urbanizing Miami area. Today numerous plans, subject to challenge by private interest and bureaucratic roadblocks, are being discussed for restoring the original flow of water from Central to South Florida, an act that would revitalize the 'Glades and, to some degree, address the often perilous water supply needs of Greater Miami.

What really sets Florida apart, though, is that it occupies a subtropical transition zone between northern temperate and southern tropical climates. This is key to the coast's florid coral-reef system, the largest in North America, and the key to Florida's prominent collection of surreal swamps, botanical oddities and monstrous critters. The Everglades

Subterranean Wonders

The national parks' caves are often overlooked by road-tripping families on summer vacations. After all, is walking around in a chilly, pitch-black tunnel really as appealing as hiking the back-country of the Great Smoky Mountains or paddling through the mangroves of the Everglades? Maybe not on the surface, but the thrill of exploring the underworld's bizarre formations should not be passed over.

Mammoth Cave in Kentucky is one of three enormous cave systems in the US that have been protected as national parks (along with Carlsbad Caverns, New Mexico, and Wind Cave, South Dakota). Rangers lead tours of Mammoth, which is the world's largest known cave system, with over 400 miles of labyrinths. If you're interested in spelunking, sign up for their challenging Wild Cave Tour.

gets the most press, and as an International Biosphere, World Heritage Site and national park, this 'river of grass' deserves the attention, while the Keys are dollops of intensely beautiful mangrove forest biomes.

Northern & Western Florida

The peninsula's north and west is also host to some remarkable landscapes. The white-sand beaches of the Gulf Coast have been gently lapped over geological millennia into wide sugary ribbons studded with prehistoric shells. The Panhandle's Apalachicola River basin has been called a 'Garden of Eden,' in which ice-age plants survive in lost ravines, and where more species of amphibians and reptiles hop and slither than anywhere else in the US. The Indian River Lagoon estuary, stretching 156 miles along the Atlantic Coast, is the most diverse on the continent. And across North Florida, the pockmarked and honeycombed limestone (called karst terrain) holds the Florida aquifer, which is fed solely by rain and bubbles up like liquid diamond in more than 700 freshwater springs.

The South

The peaks in the Southern Appalachians are the highest in the Appalachian range, topping out at Mt Mitchell (6684ft) in North Carolina. Nearby, the wet, heavily forested Great Smoky Mountains is the US's most-visited national park, with 16 summits over 5000ft. Steep elevation gradients, deep V-shaped valleys, ridges, abundant rainfall and high summertime humidity make the Appalachians one of the most diverse ecosystems in all of North America.

Heading south, things get wetter and warmer, passing through the floodplain forests in South Carolina's Congaree, famous for its large tracts of old-growth deciduous forest.

Behind the Scenes

Acknowledgements

Climate map data adapted from Peel MC, Finlayson BL & McMahon TA (2007) 'Updated World Map of the Köppen-Geiger Climate Classification', *Hydrology and Earth System Sciences*, 11, pp1633–44.

Cover photograph: Alligators, Everglades, Christophe Papke/Getty Images ©

This Book

This 1st edition of Lonely Planet's *Florida & the South's National Parks* was researched and written by Anthony Ham, Amy Balfour, Loren Bell, Greg Benchwick, Jade Bremner, Jennifer Rasin Denniston, Michael Grosberg, Bradley Mayhew, Carolyn McCarthy, Christopher Pitts and Regis St Louis.

This guidebook was produced by the following:

Commissioning Editor Angela Tinson
Product Editor Barbara Delissen
Book Designer Virginia Moreno
Assisting Editors Nigel Chin, Paul Flood, Michael MacKenzie
Cartographer Hunor Csutoros
Cover Researcher Hannah Blackie
Thanks to Ronan Abayawickrema , Imogen Bannister, Alex Conroy, Andrea Dobbin, Sasha Drew, Sonia Kapoor

Send Us Your Feedback

We love to hear from travelers – your comments keep us on our toes and help make our books better. Our well-traveled team reads every word on what you loved or loathed about this book. Although we cannot reply individually to postal submissions, we always guarantee that your feedback goes straight to the appropriate authors, in time for the next edition. Each person who sends us information is thanked in the next edition.

Visit lonelyplanet.com/contact to submit your updates and suggestions or to ask for help. Our award-winning website also features inspirational travel stories and news.

Note: We may edit, reproduce and incorporate your comments in Lonely Planet products such as guidebooks, websites and digital products, so let us know if you are happy to have your name acknowledged. For a copy of our privacy policy visit lonelyplanet.com/legal.

A – Z

Index

A

accommodations 13, 21
activities 32-3, 116-20, *see also individual activities*
alligators 29, 43, 51
Alum Cave Bluffs 66, **66**
Amicalola Falls State Park 80
amphibians 123-4
Anhinga Trail 48
animals 6, 28-9, 121-4, *see also individual animals*
Antiquities Act 114
Appalachian Trail 6, 24-5, 80-5
Asheville 78
Atlanta 98

B

bald cypress 45, 125
Bear Creek Mound 92
bears 29, 43, 122
Big Cypress Preserve 52
Biltmore Estate 78-9
birds 123
bird-watching 16, 123
Birmingham 101
Biscayne National Park 5, 22-3, 29, 38-9, **39**
black bears 29, 43, 122
Blowing Rock 75
Blue Ridge Parkway 24-5, 27, 31, 74-9, **75**
boat tours 52, 119
boating 38
books 17
Boone 74
Burmese python 109

C

Cades Cove 60-1
canoeing & kayaking 118-19
   Biscayne National Park 38
   Congaree National Park 9, 33, 58
   Everglades 4, 33, 48-9, 50, 52-3
   Flamingo 50
   Hot Springs 83
   Mammoth Cave National Park 97
   Natchez Trace Parkway 92
Carmichael, Stokely 102
Carvers Gap 84
caves 8, 31, 96, 132
Charlies Bunion 72-3, **73**
Chickasaw Village 93-4
children, travel with 30-1
Civil Rights movement 98-105
Civilian Conservation Corps (CCC) 113
climate 12, 14-16
   Florida 36
   southern USA 56
climate change 109, 127
Clingmans Dome 9, 82, 84
clothing 20-1
Confederate graves 92
Congaree National Park 9, 22-3, 58-9, **59**
coral reefs 5
costs 13
COVID-19 2
coyotes 122
crafts
   Folk Art Center 77
   Log Cabin Gift Shop 94
   Mississippi Craft Center 94
   Parkway Crat Center 75
cycling 63, 119

D

Dahlonega 81-2
diving & snorkeling 5, 10, 29, 39, 47, 119
dolphins 122
driving tours 24-5
   Appalachian Trail 24-5, 80-4, **81**
   Blue Ridge Parkway 24-5, 74-9, **75**
   Civil Rights Tour 24-5, 98-103, **99**
   Everglades 24-5, 50-3, **51**
   Great Smoky Mountains 31
   Natchez Trace Parkway 24-5, 90-5, **91**
   Newfound Gap Road 68, **68**
   Roaring Forks Motor Nature Trail 69, **69**
Dry Tortugas National Park 10, 22-3, 46-7, **47**

E

Elvis Presley's Birthplace 93
environmental issues 109, 127-9
equipment 20-1
events 14-16
Everglades City 52-3
Everglades National Park 4, 6, 22-3, 24-5, 29, 48-53, 109, **49**
Evers, Medgar 105

F

festivals 14-16
films 17
fishing 120
Flamingo 50
flora 29, 44, 124-6
Florida 36-53, 130-2, **37**
   climate 36
   highlights 36
   travel seasons 36

Florida City 50-1
Florida panthers 42, 121-2
Fontana Lake 31
forests 125
Fort Jefferson 46
Franklin 90-1
French Camp 94

G

galleries, *see* museums & galleries
Gatlinburg 82
geography 130-2
geology 130-2
ghost orchid 44
Grandfather Mountain 76
Great Smoky Mountains
National Park 60-71, 82, **61**
flora 125-6
highlights 5, 7, 9, 10, 29, 31
overview 22-3

H

highlights 4-11
Florida 36
southern USA 56
hiking 26-7, 116-18, 120
Alum Cave Bluffs 66, **66**
Appalachian Trail 6, 33, 80-4
Biscayne 29
Blue Ridge Parkway 27
Charlies Bunion 27, 72-3, **73**
Congaree National Park 27, 58
Everglades 29, 50
Great Smoky Mountains
National Park 27, 29, 33, 61-3
Kephart Loop 27, 72-3, **73**
Laurel Falls 67, **67**
Laurel Fork Gorge 84
Moses H Cone Memorial
Park 75
Mt Pisgah 79
safety 18-19, 118
history 110-15
Homestead 50-1

horseback riding 120
Great Smoky Mountains
National Park 64
Moses H Cone Memorial
Park 75
Hot Springs National Park 11,
22-3, 31, 83, 86-7, **87**
hurricanes 15

I

internet resources 13

J

Jeff Busby Park 94

K

kayaking, *see* canoeing & kayaking
Kephart Loop 72-3, **73**
King Jr, Dr Martin Luther 98,
99-100, 102, 105

L

Laurel Falls 67, **67**
Laurel Fork Gorge 84
Little Rock 104
Little Rock Central High School
22-3, 104
Lorraine Motel 22-3, 105
Lowndes County 102

M

Mammoth Cave National Park 8,
22-3, 31, 96-7, 132, **97**
manatees 29, 42, 123
mangroves 44, 125
maps 21
Maritime Heritage Trail 39
Max Patch Mountain 83-4
Medgar & Myrlie Evers Home
National Monument 22-3, 105
Memphis 102
Meriwether Lewis Site 91-2
Miccosukee Village 51-2
money 12

Montgomery 99-100
mountain biking 119
Mountain Crossings at
Walasi-Yi 81
Mt LeConte 61
Mt Mitchell State Park 76-7
Muir, John 112
museums & galleries
Big Cypress Gallery 52
Dahlonega Courthouse Gold
Museum 81
Dexter Avenue Parsonage 99
Folk Art Center 77
Gangster Museum of
America 86-7
King Center for Nonviolent
Social Change 98
Legacy Museum 99
Lowndes County Interpretive
Center 100
Miccosukee Indian
Museum 52
Moses H Cone Memorial
Park 75
National Civil Rights
Museum 102
National Voting Rights
Museum 100
Naturally Georgia 81
Penn Center 104
Pinball Museum 78
Rosa Parks Museum 99
Tuskegee Institute 98-9
music 17, 78

N

Nashville 90
Natchez 95
Natchez Trace Parkway 24-5,
90-5, **91**
national monuments 115
national parks overview 22-5
Native American mounds
Bynum Mounds 94
Emerald Mound 94
Pharr Mounds 92

O

Ochopee 52
Old Trace 91
otters 123

P

paddling, see canoeing & kayaking
panthers 42, 121-2
Parks, Rosa 99, 100
Penn Center 22-3, 104
planning 65
    Blue Ridge Parkway 76
    budgeting 13
    national parks basics 12-13, 22-5
plants 29, 44, 124-6
politics 108-9
Presley, Elvis 93

R

rafting 31, 119
    Great Smoky Mountains National Park 10, 63
    Hot Springs 83
reptiles 123-4
Roan Mountain State Park 84
Roaring Forks Motor Nature Trail 69, **69**

Roosevelt, Franklin Delano 113
Roosevelt, Theodore 113, 114

S

safe travel 18-19, 118
sea oats 45
sea turtles 15, 43, 124
Selma 100-1
Selma to Montgomery march 100, 102
Shark Valley 51
snakes 109, 124
snorkeling, see diving & snorkeling
southern USA 56-105, **57**
    climate 56
    highlights 56
    travel seasons 56
Springer Mountain 80
Student Nonviolent Coordinating Committee (SNCC) 102
sustainable travel 128
swamps 45, 124-5
swimming 120

T

Tishomingo State Park 92
travel within Florida & the South 13

Tupelo 93
Tupelo-Baldcypress Swamp 94
Tuskegee 98-9

V

Valle Crucis 74

W

water 19, 128
waterfalls 7
    Amicalola 80
    Cataract Falls 82
    Great Smoky Mountains 7
    Laurel Falls 67, **67**
    Linville Falls 76
    Nantahala Falls 82
    Place of a Thousand Drips 69
    Rainbow Falls 61
    Ramsay Cascades 61
    Tishomingo State Park 92
weather 12, 14-16, 36, 56
wetlands 124-5
whales 123
wi-fi 12
wildfires 62
wildflowers 14, 16
wildlife watching 50
wolves 122

Symbols & Map Key

These symbols and abbreviations give vital information for each listing:

🌿 Sustainable or green recommendation

FREE No payment required

☎ Telephone number	🏊 Swimming pool
⊙ Opening hours	🚌 Bus
P Parking	⛴ Ferry
❄ Air-conditioning	🚋 Tram
📶 Wi-fi access	🚆 Train
	👪 Family-friendly

Find your best experiences with these Great For... icons.

Beaches		📷 Photo Op	
🚲 Cycling		🔭 Scenery	
👪 Family Travel		🥾 Walking	
📖 History		❄ Winter Travel	
🐦 Wildlife			

Points of Interest

🏖 Beach	☣ Ruin
⛺ Camping	🛍 Shopping
🛶 Canoeing/Kayaking	⛷ Skiing
🍸 Drinking & Nightlife	🛏 Sleeping
🍴 Eating	🚶 Walking
🏠 Hut/Shelter	🐾 Zoo/Wildlife Sanctuary
👁 Lookout	◎ Other Sight
▲ Mountain/Volcano	✪ Other Activity
❶ Monument	● Other Point of Interest
🏛 Museum/Gallery/ Historic Building	)(Pass
🌳 Park	🍽 Picnic Area
	◒ Springs/Waterfall

Information & Transport

✈ Airport		P Parking	
⊗ Border crossing		⛽ Petrol station	
🚌 Bus		🚻 Toilet	
Cable car/Funicular		ℹ Tourist Information	
Cycling		Train station/Railway	
Detour		● Other Information/ Transport	
Ferry			
Ⓜ Metro station			

Our Story

A beat-up old car, a few dollars in the pocket and a sense of adventure. In 1972 that's all Tony and Maureen Wheeler needed for the trip of a lifetime – across Europe and Asia overland to Australia. It took several months, and at the end – broke but inspired – they sat at their kitchen table writing and stapling together their first travel guide, *Across Asia on the Cheap*. Within a week they'd sold 1500 copies. Lonely Planet was born.

Today, Lonely Planet has offices in Dublin, Beijing and Delhi, with more than 2000 contributors. We share Tony's belief that 'a great guidebook should do three things: inform, educate and amuse'.

Our Writer

Anthony Ham

Anthony is a freelance writer who travels the world in search of stories. His particular passions are the wildlife, wild places and wide-open spaces of the planet, from the Great Plains of the US to the Amazon, East and Southern Africa, and the Arctic. He writes for magazines and newspapers around the world, and his book *The Last Lions of Africa* was published in 2020.

STAY IN TOUCH LONELYPLANET.COM/CONTACT

IRELAND
Digital Depot, Digital Hub
Roe Lane (off Thomas St)
Dublin 8, D08 TCV4

 twitter.com/ lonelyplanet
 facebook.com/ lonelyplanet
 instagram.com/ lonelyplanet
 youtube.com/ lonelyplanet
 lonelyplanet.com/ newsletter